P9-DHZ-928

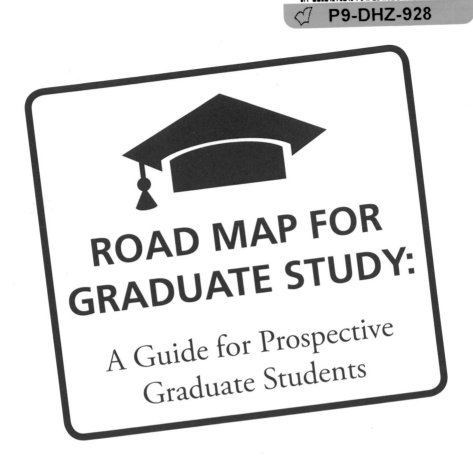

ROAD MAP FOR GRADUATE STUDY:

A Guide for Prospective Graduate Students

Donald C. Martin

*Dedicated to all of the students with whom
it has been my privilege to work*

Copyright© 2008 by Dr. Donald C. Martin, Ph.D.

All rights reserved. No part of this book may be reproduced or transmitted
in any form or by any means, electronic or mechanical, including photocopying,
recording, or by any information storage and retrieval system,
without permission in writing from the author or his heirs.

CONTENTS:

FOREWORD:

"Hello…congratulations…and best wishes…" Thus begins this succinct, yet wonderfully comprehensive book – *Road Map for Graduate Study. Road Map* is actually an interactive guidebook between you, the reader, and the author, Dr. Don Martin, your knowledgeable and well-traveled tour guide. Noting the historic places and main events related to pursuing a graduate degree, Martin also brings to your attention the side-roads, the mile-markers, and even some of the possible potholes to avoid.

Why this book, and why now? According to the 2000 US Census, the median annual earnings of a bachelor degree holder are $42,877, while those of an advanced degree holder are $55,242. Now if this does not get your attention, according to the *US News* and *World Report* (Clark, 2008), the average employee with a master's degree earns 25% more than a worker who holds a bachelor's degree, and a professional degree can double, on average, the earnings of a bachelor degree holder. And those are just the financial benefits that are possible from completing graduate studies. The intrinsic and interpersonal rewards can actually be even more advantageous. So, let's say that you're now interested, yet wondering, how do you get from this point to getting started?

I was a classroom student for a total of 20 years, and have been in an academic leadership role as a Dean or a Vice President for more than 15 years, so I have spent over half of my life thus far in school! While I have, therefore, greatly benefited from the expertise of admission officers and enrollment managers, I have never taken the time to carefully study and delineate the steps to move from the pre-application stage, through admittance, and to ending (i.e., degree completion). In a writing style that is conversational and accessible, *Road Map* carefully lays out the entire process in a steady flow of facts and also acknowledges the associated feelings that they can evoke, interweaving the author's professional and personal perspectives.

Now, I suspect that many of you have never been in Don Martin's gentle, reassuring presence. And since this is his first published book, it's safe for me to speculate that most readers of this book have never before even heard of Don Martin. Well, I have, and in *Road Map*, I could actually hear Don's voice as he offers experience-based guidance, anticipates questions that you may not even realize you have, and suggests an array of possible "answers" for you to consider.

Through a balance of linearity and iteration, cycling backwards and forward with additional information, queries, and tips, this book makes accessible and humanizes a journey that could be experienced as impersonal and even objectifying. *Road Map* reminds us that we are all individuals who must ultimately be true to who we know ourselves to be, right now.

In short, (and yes, this book is only 100 pages long!!), *Road Map for Graduate Study* wisely asserts that, regardless of your reasons, if you have the desire to pursue a graduate degree, do so and fully immerse yourself in the process throughout. As Martin acknowledges, there are always multiple paths to any one goal, and regardless of those we may select, we must at all times have as <u>one</u> of our goals, to risk living our lives most fully.

So begin…and enjoy!

Darlyne Bailey, Ph.D.
Dean and Campbell Leadership Chair
College of Education and Human Development
Assistant to the President
University of Minnesota

References:

Clark, K. (2008 March 26). How to get financial aid for grad school. US News and World Report Online. Retrieved 28 March 2008 from http://www.usnews.com/articles/education/best-graduate-schools/2008/03/26/how-to-get-financial-aid-for-grad-school.html

US Census Bureau, Housing and Household Economic Statistics Division (2005 May 13). Table 1. Employment, Work Experience, & Earnings by Age & Education. Civilian Noninstitutional Population. Data from 2000 Census. Retrieved 28 March 2008 from http://www.census.gov/hhes/www/income/earnings/call1usboth.html

INTRODUCTION:

Hello. I am guessing that you have picked up, purchased or borrowed this book because you are thinking about pursuing a graduate degree of some sort - most likely a master's or doctoral degree. Congratulations for even thinking about doing this! And, best wishes as you continue on with the process of preparing for, and then earning, your degree.

For most prospective graduate students there is both a sense of excitement and a degree of apprehension associated with the graduate school admissions process, as well as with succeeding once enrolled in graduate school. While your undergraduate educational choice was most likely a joint venture with those who had a certain degree of authority and influence over you, such as family members, high school personnel, etc., the decision about when and where to attend graduate school is, for the most part, yours alone. You may have a sense of excitement about that. However, there may also be a sense of nervousness as you contemplate "getting in," and once admitted, how you will handle everything, especially the financial obligations.

It may be helpful to know that in addition to being an enrollment management professional, I have been in your shoes twice. In 1983, I completed a two-year master's degree program. Twelve years later I earned a Ph.D., which took six years to complete. In both instances, I started as a full-time student and completed my degree part-time after returning to the world of employment. While the challenges and sacrifices were many, so were and continue to be the rewards – personally, professionally and financially.

While not initially aspiring to a career in enrollment management, I have spent 28 years meeting and recruiting prospective students, evaluating their applications, working with them as students, and watching them move from matriculation to graduation. During this time I have seen and in some cases done interviews for quite a few books and articles written about the graduate admissions process. These publications were written by individuals who may have gone through the process at some point but who have not made a career of enrollment management. I believe I have something to offer from an "insider's" perspective that can help you understand what happens on the other side of the process. You will be the final determinant of that after reading this book.

My thoughts/observations/suggestions are organized as follows: Chapter One focuses on the search process – the starting point for graduate study. Chapter Two moves in to the actual application process. Chapter Three addresses a few points about the student experience. Finally, in Chapter Four I respond to some Frequently Asked Questions (FAQs) of inquirers, applicants, admitted students and those enrolled in graduate study.

Brevity is something I value most of the time. My communication style tends to be rather short on words. Therefore, this is not a 1,000-page volume that delves fully in to every possible nuance of searching about, applying for, and completing a graduate degree. Rather, I have focused my attention on discussing certain (and what I believe to be very important) issues that have been part of my work in the admissions/financial aid/student services/career placement business. Where applicable, I will provide examples of what I am suggesting and/or describing from the host of experiences I've encountered in my work. Finally, I provide opportunities for you to answer some questions as you move from chapter to chapter.

Happy reading! May your educational dreams become realities.

Donald C. Martin
January, 2008

I want to thank the following individuals for their assistance to me in the preparation of this book:

◆ Jarred Garber and Diane Canestra from Bentley Graphics. How can I ever thank you for the amazing work you did and the tremendous help you provided? You are consummate professionals!!

◆ Allison Modica from T2AP Creative Team. Thank you for your outstanding editorial assistance.

◆ Darlyne Bailey. You are my mentor and friend. Thank you for everything.

Tom Rock, Mora Sorial and Iraida Torres-Irizarry. Thank you for the extremely helpful comments on Chapter One (Mora), Chapter Two (Tom and Iraida) and Chapter Four (Tom). Your feedback was invaluable.

Debbie and Daron, Don and Kelly, Natasha, Katie, Donna and Dan, and Kim. You are the best! Thanks for your input on the cover design - Donna and Dan, thanks for looking over the manuscript too! Most of all, thanks for your support. I love you very much.

Toni, Lucy, Roger, Lionel and Helen, Bob and Mary Lou, Leslie, Merilyn, and Marcile and Pete. You are so very thoughtful. Thanks for your feedback and support. I love you.

Pedro, Sally, Linda, Donna and Linda, Marianne, Maria, Tony and Miguel, Daryl, Sunny and RoseAnn. Thanks for your friendship. It means the world to me.

Wayne Palmer and Heidi von Schwedler from Palmer Multimedia Imaging. Thank you for a great photo shoot.

Lancaster Bible College. Thank you for giving me my start in higher education.

Wheaton College, Northwestern University, The University of Chicago and Columbia University. Thank you for providing me with some amazing employment opportunities, and in addition, for helping me develop as a higher education practitioner.

Brendan Martin Collins, my godson. You are such a special part of my life. I love you.

Esther Sprecher Martin, my mother. I will be eternally grateful for your unconditional love, unending encouragement and unparalleled support. I wish you were here to witness the publication of this book. You are the wind beneath my wings. I love and miss you so very much.

CHAPTER 1

GETTING STARTED
(The Search Process)

CHAPTER 1

GETTING STARTED
(The Search Process)

As you begin your search for the right graduate program, the first thing you need to do is make and take the time you need to do an effective job. This chapter has three sections: 1) Seven Personal Questions to ask yourself; 2) A special word on allowing enough time for your search; 3) A twelve-month check list which begins with all of your graduate school options and ends with your being ready to make application to those institutions you have selected.

Seven Personal Questions to Ask Yourself

At some point in your recent past you have decided to consider graduate study. You may or may not end up going in that direction, but for now it is on your mind. Before going any further, ask yourself the following seven questions:

1. **Why do you want to do this? There are many reasons. Here are some:**

    ❍ To truly learn more

    ❍ To add a credential to your resume

    ❍ To have a better chance of being promoted

    ❍ To have more credibility in your chosen field

    ❍ To change careers

    ❍ To increase your earning potential

    ❍ Because of pressure from your family

    ❍ Because of a need to feel better about yourself

    ❍ Because you don't know what else to do at the moment

    ❍ Something else

What are my reasons for pursuing a graduate degree?

(+) add credential to my resume. (+) Get a better job. (+) more money (+) because I am not ready to get a real job yet. (+) I want to be able to get a job where I won't be stuck inside all day.

Do my reasons make sense? Yes, they are all sensable & basicly work toward the goal of getting a job I would love.

2. Why do you want to do this now?

○ Because you're mentally/emotionally ready for a new challenge

○ Because your employer is encouraging you to do so, and might help sponsor you

○ Because you have reached a plateau in your career

○ Because you are not getting any younger

○ Because it is a logical next step for you professionally

○ Because you are ready financially

○ Because you have the necessary time to commit

○ Something else

Why do I want to pursue a graduate degree now? (+) because I am coming right out of my BS & I don't want a break in schooling. I am afraid I won't go back. (+)I want to finish school & be settled into a life before I start a family.

14

Do my reasons make sense? _Yes. Although full_
of aprehension, I think it is
reasonable.

3. **What type of academic/professional degree are you seeking?**

at least ⊗ M.A., <u>M.S.</u>, J.D., MBA, MSW, MSJ, M.Ed., etc.,

maybe ⊗ Ed.D., <u>Ph.D.</u>, LL.M., M.D., Psy.D., etc.

○ Joint degree

If you are seeking a degree in law, medicine, or business, you have a fairly clear idea of the type of professional graduate degree you need. However, if you are thinking about education, social service, public policy, the humanities, social sciences, etc., you may want to do a more thorough search of the type of degree earned for the area in which you are interested. For example, you may not need a Ph.D. to advance in the area of public policy; a master's degree may be sufficient.

What type of degree am I seeking? _I want at_
least a MS., maybe a Ph.D.
I will have to check jobs to
see what is required

4. **Is there a geographic region of your country or the world where you would like to study?**

Perhaps you have always wanted to live in another part of your country or go abroad for graduate study. Knowing what you are thinking as to location will help guide your search. However, at this early stage be careful not to rule out a certain location completely. During the search process, you may find that an option emerges in that geographic region that may be worth a closer look.

Where would I like to study? _I am open to anything, but would love a warm part of the country most._

5. What type of learning/student experience are you looking for?

Do you want an environment where faculty and students have an interactive learning approach? Are you more interested in a lecture style? Do you want to have a lot of social interaction with fellow students outside the classroom? Are you going to focus primarily on your coursework? Do you have a preference of studying at a more research-oriented institution? Do you prefer a public or private college/university?

What type of learning/student experience do I want? _I want a hands on learning experience. I want a good school moral, diversity is important. I would like a good mix of research/classroom exp._

6. If a significant other/child(ren) are going to be impacted by your plans, how are you involving them in the search process?

Graduate students with partners/children have an additional responsibility/added dimension when thinking about graduate study. All are impacted by the experience. Adjustments need to be discussed, anticipated and managed. Please do not leave this important part of your planning unattended. Building a sense of consensus and excitement with all involved in the experience will reap huge dividends when the inevitable rough spots appear on the journey. To that end it is important for you to consider the next question.

7. Should you consider a full-time or part-time program?

Most graduate degree programs can be pursued on a full- or part-time basis. There are pros and cons for both. Going full-time means finishing more quickly, but also means a possible change in employment status and income. As for the student experience, full-time students tend to develop more of a social network, which translates into continued personal and professional relationships after graduation. Part-time students are usually juggling the demands of their studies with employment obligations. This does not allow much time for socializing and developing networks. However, the benefits of employment tend to lessen the pressure of finances.

Are the significant others in my life involved in the decision-making process with me?

☒ Yes ○ No

Am I leaning toward

☒ Full-time? ○ Part-time?

Allow Enough Time for Your Search

Having considered these questions, you are now ready to start gathering information about the various options available to you. Allow time for your search. Graduate school is not something to take lightly. As we have just observed, it involves a major investment personally, intellectually, socially, emotionally, and financially. Be sure to allow yourself enough time to do your "due diligence" and get all of the information you want and need. It is wise to take about a year to do your research. If you are considering starting your program of study in the fall, you will want to start your search two years ahead of time. Why two years, you may ask? Typically, graduate schools start accepting applications just under a year before the intended start date. In order for you to have time to thoroughly evaluate all of the information you will receive and read, you will need at least a year before applying to gather that information and thoroughly review it.

Monthly Checklist for Your Search

Twelve months before applying:

 Answer the seven personal questions posed at the beginning of this chapter.

Do an initial web-based search on graduate programs, based on the answers to your personal questions. For example, if you have decided on a part-time program and know where you would like to study, do a search of educational institutions that offer a part-time program in the area and degree classification you desire. You can also do a search by program, such as Psychology, Law, Humanities, Advertising, Finance, etc. Make sure you do a couple of searches, so as many institutions matching your search criteria as possible are found.

Once you have done a thorough search, make an alphabetical list of all your options, regardless of what you presently know/have heard about them. Write them all down or put them on a spreadsheet. **REMEMBER: PERCEPTION IS REALITY – IT'S WHERE YOU END UP, NOT WHERE YOU START.** Be very careful about accepting word of mouth or what you think you know as final at this point in the search process. We are individuals, and as such, have different needs, expectations and experiences. This is YOUR educational experience – not someone else's. You need to start by gathering a list of options. Do not eliminate any of them at this point. You want to get as much information as possible so you can decide what options are most appealing.

○ Go online and do some initial research on all the institutions you have on your list. Assess not only the content of material on websites, but look at the way in which it is presented. Is information easy to find? Is the tone friendly and inviting? Are there easy and quick ways to request more information? Speaking of which, this would be a good time to request written information from each of the institutions. This will enable you to review what you receive any time you want. It will also provide you an opportunity to find out just how responsive admissions offices are to you. This can be very telling, and may shed light on the general level of responsiveness of those institutions about which you have made inquiry. Give each institution a grade on their website, and on the level of responsiveness they provided to you. Here is a suggested grading system:

Website

A = easy to navigate, informative, captivating
B = well-done, good information, friendly
C = fairly easy to navigate, not as helpful/friendly
D = difficult to navigate, not very informative
F = what were they thinking?
FF = no website, or close to nothing

Responsiveness

A = had a response within 7 business days
B = had a response within 12 business days
C = had a response within 17 business days
D = had a response within 22 business days
F = took three weeks or longer for a response
FF = no response

○ Should you consider taking a graduate level course or two now? Perhaps you were an undergraduate student awhile ago, or you may have received your bachelor's degree very recently. Either way, if your undergraduate GPA was not what you believe is competitive, or does not speak to the academic work you believe you are capable of performing, you would do well to register at a nearby institution as a non-degree student and take one or two courses. If you do, earning an A or B will be very impressive to the admissions committee, and will demonstrate that you are able to perform well as a student.

TIP: *This is a good time to start setting aside financial resources for your search and application process. There will be standardized tests and application fees for sure. In addition, you may decide to purchase some test taking preparation materials and/or to visit some of the institutions you end up placing on your list of top options.*

Eleven months before applying:

○ Based on the two items above (website and responsiveness), you are now in a position to narrow your search a bit. But do not narrow it too much. Obviously those institutions you have graded as F or FF could most likely be eliminated. You may be surprised at some of the options you are eliminating should you rely completely on the grades given. If you still have an interest in a college/university that you did not initially grade well, keep it on the list for now. However, if you continue to get the same treatment you did when first browsing the web and/or asking for information, ask yourself the following question: If I'm being treated this way now, how will it be should I apply, be offered admission, and enroll?

○ Create a research spreadsheet to use from this point on for each of the options that remain on your list. You may have already started a spreadsheet when you did your initial research. If so, you are just expanding it now. If not, this is the time to start one. Down the left hand column will be an alphabetical list of your options. Across the top will be all of the areas about the options that you want to compare. Here are some suggestions:

a. Website grade
b. Responsiveness grade
c. Usefulness of printed materials/brochures
d. Friendliness of admissions staff
e. Interaction with current students
f. Interaction with faculty
g. Interaction with alumni
h. Campus visit/Admissions event(s) you attended
i. Number of students enrolled in the entire institution
j. Number of students enrolled in the program you are considering
k. Professor/student ratio
l. Average class size
m. Grading system
n. Facilities
o. Housing options (should you be re-locating)

p. Extracurricular opportunities
q. Career services/employment percentages
r. Total cost of education for one year
s. Tuition cost for one year
t. Financial Aid – scholarships, loans, assistantships, fellowships, work study
u. Application deadlines
v. Application fees
w. Application requirements (including what standardized test(s) are needed)
x. Must you do an interview?
y. Do they keep a waiting list of applicants?
z. Can you appeal/get feedback if denied?

TIP: *Some of the columns in your research spreadsheet will have letter grades, some will say "yes," "no" or "maybe," some will be dates, dollar amounts or various numerical responses, and some will be more evaluative (scale of 1-5, with 1 being terrible and 5 being outstanding).*

Ten months before applying:

○ Work on completing your research spreadsheet, filling in every column for each option. As you go along you will eliminate a few or quite a few. That is okay. As a consumer you are doing what you should be doing – comparison shopping.

○ After reviewing your entire spreadsheet, do a very general rank order of the options that remain. You could rank every option, starting with #1 and going to the end of the list. Or, you could group your options: top group, second group, third group, etc. Whenever possible, you should have at least five options left. Hopefully, you will have many more. However, depending on the type of graduate program you seek, the number of options will vary. My point is that you are still not at the place where you need to have a "short list." You are still ten months away from applying, and will have several opportunities to narrow down your list before that time.

○ Take a look at the general rank order you have done. Do you believe the ranking is based on what YOU really feel? Did you get enough information to complete your ranking?

TIP: *Remember, you can and should feel free to change your research spreadsheet evaluations at any time. Perhaps further information and/or contact with one or more of your options will cause them to go up or down on your overall list. That is another great reason for taking plenty of time do to your research. You tend to learn more about an institution the longer you do research about it. First impressions, while important, may change later on based on repeated observation and communication.*

Nine months before applying:

○ Start thinking about making some campus visits. It is one thing to review a website, read printed materials and communicate with admissions office staff on the phone or via email. It is quite another thing to actually visit a campus in person. Most institutions offer a variety of campus visit programming, usually described on their website. Here is a good tip: If you can afford to visit an institution more than once, make your first visit unannounced. This will help you get a feeling for what the institution is really like. How you are treated as a "complete stranger" can be very revealing. If, however, you do not have the time and/or funds to do more than one visit, you may want to wait for your visit until you have started the application process. More about this in Chapter Two.

○ Start preparing for any standardized tests required as part of the application process. Most graduate school admissions committees will require the GRE, GMAT, LSAT, MCAT, or another test. In addition, if you enroll at an institution in another country, and the primary language in that country is different from your own, you will most likely be required to take a test to demonstrate your level of proficiency in that primary language.

○ There are quite a few materials available to help you prepare for these tests. You will most likely learn about these materials from the Educational Testing Service, the Graduate Management Admission Council, the Law School Admission Council and the Association of American Medical Colleges. These organizations have preparation materials available on their websites. Other organizations, such as Barrons, Kaplan, Peterson's, and the Princeton Review offer test preparation classes. In addition, you can go to your local bookstore and find a host of printed materials and study guides.

TIP: *Standardized tests bring varying degrees of stress for prospective students. Obviously, some individuals do better on these tests than others. While test scores measure a certain level of academic ability, they by no means cover the entire academic arena. Most admissions committees do not have a cut-off requirement for test scores, but some do. It is a good idea to find out what each of your options looks for and requires.*

Eight months before applying:

○ Now is the time to do some additional research on your options. One area that may be of interest is the type of press they receive. There are at least two ways to find this out: One is to go the website and look for a link that might read: "(institution name) in the news," or "press coverage of (institution name)." A second way is to log on to a search engine on the web, and look for press coverage. Conducting this type of search will yield more news clips than would be found on an institution's website. This is because institutional websites tend to accentuate only positive press coverage.

○ Another way to learn about your options is to read their institutional and student-run newspapers. In some cases you may have to ask for these by mail, and in other cases you can access them on a website. This allows you to review both external (press) and internal (institutional/student) perspectives (faculty, research, etc.), which you will not find in admissions or other promotional information.

○ Find out if there are rankings of institutions offering the graduate program you are seeking. Various organizations provide annual or bi-annual rankings that can be useful to you. However, REMEMBER: RANKINGS AND REPUTATION ARE TWO DIFFERENT THINGS. Organizations that do rankings may try to provide reliable information, but those actually doing the data gathering, analysis, and dissemination of the rankings have biases of their own. Often times they have never stepped foot on campus. Also, rankings provide a source of revenue for the organizations doing them. One ranking differs from the next. And, by the time you enroll in graduate school, the ranking of your options will most likely have changed. It will change again while you are enrolled and yet again after you graduate. So you need to be very careful how much you allow a ranking to influence your final decision about where to apply. You may be better off looking for trends, such as: Has a particular institution been consistently ranked in the top 20?

○ At this point do a second evaluation of your options, considering what you have discovered from external and internal press and rankings. Remember, you are not ready to make your short list yet. You can, however, change your spreadsheet evaluations at any time. It also may be that something you learn from the press or rankings about an option that was eliminated earlier from your list may cause you to place that option back on.

TIP: *REMEMBER: RANKINGS AND YOUR SUCCESS IN AND AFTER GRADUATE SCHOOL ARE ALSO TWO DIFFERENT THINGS. Your ultimate success will depend on YOU, not on the ranking of your graduate degree-granting institution. Perhaps the higher the rank, the more doors might initially open up to you. But as I will discuss in Chapter Three, there are only two qualities you need to succeed, which come from within.*

Seven months before applying:

○ Contact current students at the institutions on your list. If you know someone who is attending, contact them and ask some questions. If not, ask the admissions staff if they can put you in touch with a current student. Many admissions offices have student volunteers who are willing to talk with prospective students. If you can ask the same questions for each of your options, you will have more information for purposes of comparison shopping.

○ Continue making plans for campus visits. These are best done once you have gathered the information you have so far. More about this when we discuss six months before applying.

TIP: *Prospective students greatly value contact with current students when doing their graduate school search. This may go without saying, but current students will usually give it to you straight — they have nothing to lose by sharing their "real" experiences with you and their input/comments can be of tremendous value.*

Six months before applying:

○ Make a few campus visits. You can visit unannounced, as we mentioned earlier. In addition, institutions usually offer two ways to visit campus. Both will most likely appear on the website for each institution and under the section dealing with applying, and are as follows:

    a. Most institutions provide opportunities to visit during the academic year. Visitors can usually attend classes, take a campus tour, meet current students and talk with someone in the admissions office. If an admissions interview is required as part of the application process, have the interview as part of your visit.

    b. Some institutions also have special campus visit programs, which include sessions on the admissions process, financial aid, housing, student life, career services and more. Most often, these special programs take place in the fall.

○ Another way to have a "campus visit" is to find out if admissions information sessions (also called receptions) are being held close to where you live. Many institutions recruit in areas they have identified as strong or developing markets. This provides a great way to get to know the institution better, especially if you are not able to go there for a visit.

○ If possible, divide things in such a way that between campus visits and local admissions presentations, you will be able to "visit" all of your options before applying.

○ Make sure to evaluate your visit on your spreadsheet as soon as possible after it is completed, so that your experiences and impressions will be fresh in your mind.

TIP: *ALWAYS REMEMBER: PERCEPTION IS REALITY – IT IS WHERE YOU END UP, NOT WHERE YOU START. Reputation, rankings and reality are very different things. When it comes to reputation, while an institution may be well known or considered highly prestigious, this does not mean it has to be on your final list of options or that it has the best program for you (See my final two points at the end of this chapter). As I mentioned earlier, rankings are useful. But remember that those publishing them are looking to sell what they publish. Also, make sure you take a close look at the methodology behind the rankings. You will see that some methodologies are sound while others are lacking. If an institution is ranked highly, but the methodology is not credible, you need to interpret that accordingly. Also, take a look at several rankings by the same organization/publication over time. If there is a sizeable difference between one ranking and the next, is it likely that good methodology is taking a back burner to selling copies of the ranking. It is very unlikely that one institution would move up or down several places in only one or two years. Finally, it is what is real for YOU that is most important. It is your time, energy, and financial resources that are being spent.*

Five months before applying:

○ Start making plans to take whatever standardized test(s) you will need as part of the application process. On your research spreadsheet you have a column for application requirements. You should start familiarizing yourself with both the logistics of taking the tests required, as well as actually doing some practice test taking.

○ There are many resources available to assist you in preparing for your test(s). Most major bookstores have a college/grad school prep section that offers help. Also, as most graduate school applicants are asked to take the GRE, GMAT, LSAT or MCAT, there are two primary sources of information for these:

> a. The Educational Testing Service
>   in Princeton, New Jersey (GRE)
>
> b. The Graduate Management Admission Council
>   in McLean, Virginia (GMAT)
>
> c. The Law School Admission Council
>   in Newtown, Pennsylvania (LSAT)
>
> d. The Association of American Medical Colleges
>   in Washington, D.C. (MCAT)

TIP: *Some applicants are better test takers than others. I will discuss this in Chapter Two. For now, a suggestion: Should you not score as well on your test as you had hoped, take it a second, or even a third time. This does not make you look less competitive in the application process. Rather, in most cases, it demonstrates that you are trying your best to perform well on the test.*

Four months before applying:

○ Narrow your list of options down to those to which you will submit an application. You have been working on your search for eight months now and you have a very good idea of where you would like to apply.

○ Take a close look at your research spreadsheet. Which of your options have the highest evaluations, based on all of your research, campus visits you made, and/or admissions presentations you attended?

○ Obviously, there is no limit to the number of schools to which you can apply. But remember that you will need time to complete the applications. You need to know how many you can tackle, doing a good job on each one. More about this in Chapter Two.

○ Be careful about applying to only one institution. If you are absolutely certain that this is by far the only option, be absolutely sure to prepare yourself for whatever decision you receive.

TIP: *It is important for you to keep all of the information you have gathered on all of your options until you have made your decision about where you will attend and have actually enrolled there. Should plans change in some way and you decide to hold off on your graduate studies for another year or longer, or if you decide to leave the institution, you will not be starting from scratch when you resume the research process.*

Three months before applying:

○ Now it is time to make sure you have current application materials. You will most likely access applications on the web, but some schools may still prefer that you send part or all of the application via regular mail. Having reviewed the information on your spreadsheet, you should be generally familiar with the deadlines you will need to meet for your applications.

○ Make sure to verify the requirements for admissions interviews (if applicable) and to revisit the interview deadlines for each option (You should already have some of this information on your research spreadsheet.).

○ If you have not already done so, start thinking about who you will ask to write letters of recommendation for you. If you are applying to several schools, be sure to have more than one or two individuals selected. If they are going to do a good job for you, they will need time to work on their recommendations. A good rule of thumb is: One person could probably do two or three recommendations. Once you have selected those you would like to use, contact them and get their approval.

○ Similar to the spreadsheet you created when initially doing research on your options, create an application spreadsheet. Place the names of each of your options alphabetically down the left hand column. Across the top place the items you want to be sure you remember, or compare, throughout the application process. Some of those items will include:

a. Application deadlines
b. The deadline by which you will apply
c. Ease of completing the application –
   i.e., user friendly technology?
d. Date you actually send in your application
e. Interview requirements
f. The date you scheduled your interview
g. Is the interview to be conducted on campus, in your area, by phone?
h. The date of your interview
i. Once conducted, your opinion of the interview questions, and of your interviewer
j. Were you notified that your application had been received? If so, how long after you sent it in?
k. Your rating of the contact with the admissions staff between the time you applied and the time a decision was communicated to you
l. Did the admissions office meet its deadline to notify you of a decision?

m. If admitted, how was the follow-up afterward? Too much? Too little?
n. What is the enrollment deposit amount and deadline, if admitted?
o. What information do you need for financial aid purposes, if admitted?
p. Is there a campus visit program for newly admitted students?
q. If yes, and you attended, what did you think? Is this a place at which you would feel comfortable?
r. Were you "pursued" after admission? Do you really feel wanted?
s. If wait listed, how were you treated?
t. If denied, how were you treated?
u. Is deny or re-application feedback available?
v. If you chose to appeal your denial, was the admissions staff friendly and caring?

TIP: *This is a great time to create outlines of the essays you will write. Jotting down notes for each question is extremely valuable and helps to ensure you answer questions fully. This also helps to ensure you answer the right questions for the right schools.*

Two months before applying:

○ Start completing your applications. Set aside time each day, or every other day, to do this. That way, you get a little done each time and lessen your chances of feeling overwhelmed, rushing, and/or making mistakes.

○ Address or complete one essay each time you work on your applications. This helps to spread things out and not leave you out of time later on.

○ Make sure your recommenders are ready to go with their letters/forms, and confirm that you have provided them all the information they need.

○ Start requesting transcripts. Most universities are completely familiar with this part of the application process and have very efficient procedures in place.

○ Make sure you are ready to schedule any interviews you plan to conduct. Admissions offices will have different procedures for these and you want to make sure you are following the right guidelines for the right school. Having your application spreadsheet is very helpful here.

TIP: *With the exception of essays, it may be helpful to complete the same section for each application you are submitting. That way you are going over the same information, and have a sense of accomplishment. For example, completing the demographic section for each of your applications lets you move on knowing this section is done for all of them.*

One month before applying:

○ Now it is time to fine-tune your applications. Thoroughly re-check your essays. Then have someone else check them. Go over each of the other sections to be sure you have accurately and correctly answered all questions. Check for mistakes. Then have another person check for mistakes.

○ Be certain, to the best of your ability, your applications are exactly the way you want them to be.

○ Start preparing your application fees. If sending a check, make sure you have the money to cover it. Bounced checks do not a good first impression make!

TIP: *There is a fine line between conscientiously reviewing your applications, and obsessing about perfection. We are all human. Admissions committees are not looking for perfection; they are looking for proof that an applicant took time to prepare his/her materials.*

Two Final Notes

In this chapter you have not been advised to create a concrete rank order of those institutions to which you will apply. That is deliberate. You still have another year of contact with those institutions on your list, which could greatly affect your opinion of your options. You would best be served to keep an open mind as you go through the application process.

Second, try not to get too caught up with the prestige factor of a graduate school. While graduating from a highly recognized program may initially open some doors for you, ultimately your success will depend on who you are and what you bring to the table, not on where you received your education. I know whereof I speak: My bachelor's degree was earned at an institution dictated by my family culture. Likewise, my master's degree came from a less prestigious institution. My success has largely been due to hard work, persistence and a bit of luck along the way, as opposed to where I attended college and graduate school. The credentials are important, but they do not make you what/who you are – you alone do that.

CHAPTER 2

GETTING IN
(The Application Process)

CHAPTER 2

GETTING IN
(The Application Process)

For approximately twelve months now, you have been engaged in a thorough search for the best graduate study options. Now it is time to move to the very important work of finalizing your applications, eventually submitting them for review and evaluation. Over the past year you were the consumer – you were researching, comparing and evaluating options. And you will be the consumer once again, after you receive notification from the admissions committee(s).

However, at this point in the process the tables turn. Those graduate schools to which you apply become the consumer. Now they get to research and evaluate you, and to compare you with others who have applied for admission. And while their ability to do that depends in part on them (the application evaluation process they have put in place), it also depends especially on you (how well you have presented yourself).

In this Chapter I will share some thoughts and insights about completing your application(s), and also about how to respond once you have been notified of a decision. There are three sections: 1) Pointers and tips for completing your application(s); 2) What to do if you are placed on a waiting list, denied or admitted; 3) Making the decision about where to enroll.

Seven General Pointers for Completing Applications

1. **RELAX!!**

   Do your best to relax as you work on your applications. Worrying and obsessing, while tempting, will not help. In fact, worrying and obsessing could hinder your ability to think clearly and focus on preparing the best applications you can. In truth, going through a graduate school application process can result in a major learning experience for you. As you complete each application you will engage in personal reflection and self discovery. This can prove to be very rewarding, whatever the decisions you receive from the admissions committee. As they have moved through this process, some applicants decide not to pursue graduate study or to wait awhile. Others decide to pursue an entirely different area of study than they originally had in mind.

So, use this application process to your benefit; consider it a positive learning experience in and of itself. Be calm. Be reflective. Be thoughtful. Relax.

2. **Allow time.**

If you have been following some or most of the suggestions provided in Chapter One's monthly checklist you should be feeling fairly comfortable about the application deadlines you are working to meet. In fact, allowing plenty of time during the search process, which then allows you plenty of time to complete your applications, automatically helps you to relax.

Knowing you have adequate time is very comforting and, as I mentioned earlier, allows you to focus on the task at hand - doing your best on your applications.

3. **Follow directions.**

This seems like such a "no-brainer" that you may wonder why I even mention it. I do so because over the years I have truly been amazed at the number of applicants who do not follow directions. If you are one of those applicants, it raises some questions about how well you might follow policies and procedures once admitted and enrolled. Some directives may not make sense to you, but they have been provided for a reason, and you need to comply. If you are unable or unwilling to do so, you send a clear signal about yourself to the admissions committee. It is a red flag, not a green light. Let me give you a few examples:

    a. If there is a word limit for essay questions, follow it. Remember, application evaluators are reading hundreds, maybe thousands of essays. You will not get a positive response if yours is longer than it is supposed to be.

    b. If you are asked for two letters of recommendation, do not send ten. Some institutions will permit an extra recommendation, but usually no more. Honor that.

c. If an interview is conducted by invitation only, do not request one. You might mention that you hope you will have the opportunity to interview, but leave it there.

d. If an interview is highly recommended, by all means request one, and make every possible effort to follow through. More about this in the next section of this chapter.

e. If you are an international student applying to a U.S. graduate school and are required to take a test to measure your English language skills, do so. Do not argue even if you are fluent in English. If that is the case you will obviously do very well on the test, which will serve to enhance your application.

f. Do not knowingly leave a question unanswered. Make sure you have responded to everything you've been asked and that you have really addressed the questions asked of you.

g. Be careful about sending extra materials. Some applications allow for this, or will allow you to write an extra essay question. But if they do not, first check to see if it is okay for you to send extra information rather than assuming that it is okay to do so.

4. **Be professional at all times/in all dealings.**

Remember, as an applicant you are at the part of the process where you are not in the driver's seat. You are one of many applicants being compared with each other. Always present yourself in a calm, assertive and sincere manner. It is appropriate to be inquisitive about your application, but it is never to your advantage to be argumentative. Be confident but not arrogant; be kind and patient, not abrasive and demanding.

Many admissions professionals keep written records of their interactions with applicants. At one university where I was employed we used something called the "orange sheet." If we had an extremely positive or extremely negative encounter with an applicant we wrote a summary of that interaction on an orange sheet of paper and placed the sheet just inside the person's application. When it came time to make a decision on that application, the orange sheet(s) was/were very persuasive, for better or worse.

37

Actions speak louder than words. Some of the best applications on paper have been completely devalued due to the behavior of the person who prepared them.

5. **Content and presentation are both important.**

   While what you say in your application is obviously very important, so is the "look and feel" of your application. This is especially true when the institution/program to which you are applying is extremely selective and has the luxury of choosing their admitted students from a very large applicant pool. Some applications are sloppy, wrinkled and disorganized. Others are hand-written (there is absolutely NO excuse for this in the age of word processing). Some have coffee or tea stains on them. Occasionally essay questions are not sent to the right institution, and often it is clear that they were not proof read for correct grammar or spelling. Pages are out of order. Some information is not provided, or contradicts similar information provided elsewhere in the application. Applications with these kinds of presentation errors quickly become less competitive. The admissions committee tends to assume that the applicant was not really serious about this application, and they tend to respond in a similar manner.

6. **Be yourself/human/honest. Resist the temptation to lie, embellish or make excuses**

   Don't be someone you're not. At times, applicants try to make themselves look perfect. As we all know, no one is perfect. Trying to look that way can often cause application evaluators to be more suspicious than impressed. I'm not suggesting you discuss all of your weaknesses and past mistakes (which are there for all of us), but rather, that you simply be yourself. The best applications I have read are from those who were saying the following in between the lines: "This is me. I hope you will appreciate who I am, and also appreciate the level of interest I've demonstrated in your institution by completing this application. If you choose to admit me, I'll be thrilled. If you don't, I'll be okay."

   Above all, do not lie or embellish the truth. This can have disastrous effects. In my years as an application evaluator and decision maker, I have seen individuals with great talent and potential be denied admission, have their admission revoked, or be expelled after enrolling because they lied and/or embellished. If you earned a 3.2 overall GPA, don't say it was a 3.5. If you did not serve as a class officer or student leader, don't say you did. If you were not in an organization, the military, and/or the Peace Corps, don't put it on your resume. Don't write your own letters of recommendation and/or falsify the names of their authors. Don't pretend you are someone else when an admissions representative calls to speak with you. That one probably sounds a bit strange. Let me explain. When working as Director of Admissions at the University of Chicago Graduate School of Business, I would personally phone each admitted student before she/he received notification in the mail or online. Obviously, it was a win-win phone call all the way around. I often made admitted student calls on the weekends to help spread out the number of contacts I made each day. I tended not to identify myself immediately, but did so as soon as the person on the phone indicated that they were indeed the applicant. One Saturday morning I called a newly admitted male student. The gentleman who answered the phone claimed he was not the applicant. I was sure I had dialed the correct phone number, so I tried the number again a few minutes later. This time a woman answered the phone. I identified myself and asked if the applicant was there. The same gentleman, who had just answered my call a few minutes earlier, took the phone. When I asked why he lied to me about his identity, he said he thought I was making a "sales call." Upon hearing this, I informed the applicant that while the original purpose of my call was to congratulate him on his admission, I was now informing him that he was denied.

That story could be repeated more times than I care to remember. Dishonesty is such a waste – there is absolutely no need for it. Many admissions evaluators randomly screen applicants and verify information they have provided. While it is human to be tempted, don't allow yourself to yield. There is nothing to be gained, whether you are found out or not.

Finally, don't make excuses on your application. You may decide that you need to explain a lower overall GPA, a less than stellar academic record during one of the years you were in college, a break in your employment record, holding several jobs in a short period of time, etc. If there are legitimate reasons for what might seem like a blemish in your application, by all means let the admissions committee know. Perhaps you had a serious illness, lost a loved one, had a sudden financial crisis, etc. That should definitely be mentioned. Bottom line, make explanations, not excuses. The admissions committee will know the difference and your application will either be helped or hindered.

7. **Make contingency plans in case you are not admitted. Things happen for a reason.**

   In my years as an admissions director I met applicants who were so convinced that a particular institution was for them, or that this was the year they were going to attend graduate school that they did not make plans for what to do if things did not go as they hoped. Some would go so far as to inform employers and loved ones of their plans before it was advisable to do so. In some very extreme cases they moved to where their number one graduate option was located before they received a decision on their application!

   Being confident and positive is one thing. Throwing caution to the wind is another. Be prepared to be denied admission, perhaps to every one of your options, or to be placed on the waiting list by several of your options (I'll have some suggestions on how to respond if/when this happens at the end of this chapter). Also, be prepared for what you will do if you end up not attending graduate school in the year you thought, planned, prepared and hoped to.

   Being prepared for all outcomes is not a sign of lack of belief in yourself or your abilities to do graduate work. It IS a sign that you realize life does not always go the way we plan and making alternative plans is often required.

Tips on the Interview/Essays/Recommendations/Academics

1. **The Interview**

   a. If you can interview, by all means do so. This shows that you really are interested in this institution/program.

   b. An interview provides an opportunity to "lift you off the page." This is your opportunity to let the admissions committee know who you are in person, not on paper.

   c. Interviewing can make or break an application. Be professional and courteous. Directly answer the questions asked of you and have some questions of your own ready.

   d. Do some practice interviews. Make a list of possible questions you could be asked, but be careful that your responses do not sound memorized or completely scripted.

   e. In some cases, the interviewer may do a very poor job. He/she may talk only about himself/herself, may not ask any meaningful questions of you, arrive at your interview location very late, thus shortening your time together, and/or in very extreme cases, behave inappropriately (ask personal questions, flirt, or engage in some sort of harassment). If your interview does not go well and you believe that the cause has nothing to do with you, immediately contact the admissions office. Do not be accusatory or argumentative, but straightforward. Let the committee know how you feel and ask if you might be given the opportunity to re-interview.

   Along with admissions staff, recent graduates or current students may conduct interviews. Some alumni may offer to do interviews when they are not very skilled at it, or have other "issues" which cause them to be less than credible. Immediately alerting the admissions office about an interview you believe did not go well allows for an immediate response before a final decision is made on your application. If you wait to communicate your concerns until after you have been denied or wait listed, it could be interpreted as your making excuses, or looking for something/someone else to blame.

f. Some applicants become agitated if they are told they will have their interview with a current student or recent graduate. In many instances, a student or alumni interview is best. The applicant can get a true sense of what it was/is like to be part of that particular academic community. These are the individuals who can really talk about the institution/program. They can really address questions you might have about student life, academics, housing, safety, finances, social life, and much more.

2. **Essays**

   a. Answer the question – please do this! An applicant's credibility goes down very quickly when he/she submits a lengthy essay that does not really address the issue(s) raised in the question.

   b. Stay within the word limit requested. Do not yield to the temptation to take the liberty of expanding your essays. This does not impress. In fact, it lowers credibility. Application evaluators read thousands of essays. There is a reason for the word limits they have set.

   c. Check and re-check for accuracy, proper grammar and correct spelling. Do not obsess but, at the same time, do your best to ensure that your essays are the best they can be. Have someone else read them for style and accuracy.

   d. Do not have someone else write your essays! Usually there are all forms of communication between an applicant and the admissions office during the application process, some of these being electronic. If your essay writing style is vastly different from that of other of your written communication, a red flag immediately goes up. Don't lose your chance because of dishonesty – it's not worth it. You are better than that!

   e. Sometimes you are given an opportunity to complete an optional essay. If this is in the form of another question from the admissions committee, by all means, complete that essay question. If the optional essay is provided for you to complete in any way you wish, be careful. Do not repeat what has already been communicated elsewhere in the application. If you do not have anything to add, then do not add anything – leave the question unanswered. Including an optional, open-ended essay question in the application is usually done for one primary reason: to give the applicant an opportunity to provide additional information that she/he believes will truly help make the application complete. If you believe something important has been missed, this is your opportunity to provide that information. But remember, if you are going to use this question to discuss a part of your application you believe to be less competitive, do not make excuses – provide explanations.

f. Send your essays to the right admissions office. This seems like a no-brainer, but so often essays for one program are sent with the application to a different program. When this happens, your credibility immediately falls. On many occasions I would read an essay that was prepared for anther program and mistakenly sent with the application to the program for which I was making decisions. The applicant would indicate that this other program was his/her first choice! My unspoken response: "I hope you get in at the other program, because you have just been denied, or wait listed at best."

3. Recommendation Letters

a. Choose individuals you know will feel comfortable recommending you. Once again, this may seem like a no-brainer. Yet, every so often a recommendation letter is received and the person writing it recommends that the applicant not be admitted! This is the kiss of death. When I encountered a letter like this I read no further. The applicant was immediately denied.

b. Ask those who really know you well to write your recommendation letters. There seems to be a huge myth floating around the applicant world, which is: Having a well known and/or highly influential person/alumnus write a letter of recommendation will give you an edge. If this person really knows you, no problem. But if they do not, you are barking up the wrong tree. Receiving a recommendation letter from someone who met you at a dinner party or who has a close personal/professional relationship with one of your family members, but who has never spent quality time with you, lowers credibility big time. This begs the question: does this person not have close professional associations with anyone? I have denied many an applicant for whom some very famous individuals (politicians, entertainers, journalists, athletes) provided a recommendation.

c. Ask your recommenders to assess you honestly. No one is perfect, so do not try to come off that way. If your recommender gives you a perfect rating on every single dimension she/he is evaluating, you have just gone down in the eyes of the admissions committee. Most institutions want real people in their student body, not Mr. and Ms. Perfect. Those who consider themselves this way are usually arrogant, self-centered and look down their nose at everyone else. Do not allow yourself to be perceived that way. You are human like everyone else. Application evaluators are not looking for perfection – they want real people.

d. Ask recommenders to write a separate letter. This is a nice touch. The letter does not have to be terribly long, but should address, in part, some of what was completed on the recommendation form. Perhaps the recommender can comment on one or two qualities about the applicant he/she believes to be especially strong. In addition, he/she may want to comment on something that is less strong while still providing an overall endorsement of the applicant. This, coming from an individual who really knows that applicant, is a plus.

e. Make sure your recommenders write their own letters. As indicated above when talking about essays, do not write your own recommendation letters. This can be easily detected. I have had cases where an applicant did ask someone to recommend her/him, but completely wrote the recommendation letter. Worse yet, I have encountered situations where the applicant did not ask anyone to do the recommendation. She/he simply wrote the recommendation and put someone else's name and signature on it. If this is discovered (and it often is!), so long applicant. Don't do it.

f. It is always good for recommenders to provide examples of the qualities/character traits they are claiming you possess. If a recommender indicates that you are highly motivated and a self-starter, she/he should provide an example or two. Or, if you are a good leader and have great communication/people skills, it would help to know how your recommender came to hold that opinion.

g. Send only the number of letters of recommendation requested. If the limit is two, send two. If you believe you will not best present yourself without an additional letter, go ahead and send an extra one (but no more!). And be sure you have explained why you felt the extra letter was crucial. If you take it upon yourself to send extra letters with no explanation, the admissions committee may have concerns about your ability to follow directions.

4. **Academics/Standardized Tests**

a. Your academic record is what it is. If it is not what you think will be a strong suit, explain if you need to but do not make excuses. That will make things worse.

b. If you have taken a graduate course or two since graduating from college, talk about that. This is often a good idea if your undergrad GPA was not terribly good. It indicates that you are willing to take some courses to show what you are capable of now. In almost every case, applicants who do this do quite well on their coursework and make a positive impression with the admissions committee.

c. Remember, the longer you have been out of college, the less closely your academic record will be evaluated. This is because there are more recent accomplishments or employment experiences that will be part of your application. You may have even earned a graduate degree or completed a significant amount of graduate level coursework. Let your more recent achievements shine. They will help balance a less than competitive undergraduate record. However, if you have not been out of college for very long and you have an academic record you believe is not very strong, please refer to letter "a" above. If admissions committees do their job well, you will not be automatically denied because one part of your application is less competitive, and certainly not if you have adequately addressed that issue with an explanation, not an excuse.

d. Do not take your respective standardized test more than three times. Submitting scores from multiple test completions can cause the admissions committee to perceive you as desperate, obsessive, or both. You may simply be trying your level best to get the best score you can but, usually after three attempts, the results are not going to change that much. What you have demonstrated by taking the test at least more than once, or maybe twice more, is that you were trying to do your best to get a good score.

5. **One final tip** – *If there is something about your application that you want to explain further and there is not an open-ended essay question for this purpose, feel free to enclose a cover letter addressing the issue. This will be well received, provided your comments are focused and succinct.* **Bottom line:** *Do not submit an application that you believe has a hole in it that the admissions committee will find and about which questions will be raised.*

In Review: Do's and Don'ts of the Application Process

Do -	But Don't -
Read instructions carefully	Rush
Apply when you are ready	Sacrifice quality for speed
Make a visit to the campus	Rely solely on websites/printed information
Evaluate customer service	Forget that you too are being evaluated
Be assertive	Be arrogant or argumentative
Be confident	Be conceited
Be persistent	Be a pest
Be yourself	Try to fit some sort of fake image
Lighten up and enjoy the process	Act as if this is "do or die"
Put your best foot forward	Yield to the temptation to embellish or lie

Responding to the Notification Decision

You have now submitted your application(s) and within a few weeks/months, you will start receiving notification from each admissions committee. These days you are usually able to go online to learn of the decision. In some cases, institutions notify applicants only via regular mail. In other instances you will be notified both ways by the admissions office.

The three decisions typically rendered are: Admission, Denial, or placement on a Waiting List. Rarely an applicant will be admitted conditionally. This usually means that he/she is asked to do some additional work (added essays, retaking a standardized test, taking a course or two), the successful completion of which automatically means admission.

Below are some suggestions for responding to each of the three major notification decisions. I am starting with the decision I believe can be the most difficult - being placed on a Waiting List. Then I will discuss responses to being denied and, finally, how to respond when admitted.

1. **Wait Listed** – In some ways, this is the hardest initial decision – you still don't know anything one way or the other. "Wait" often feels/sounds like a four letter word. But don't despair. Accept this decision, and consider doing the following:

   a. Don't take it personally. This is so much easier to say than to do. No one likes to be told they have been put on a waiting list. Most likely, this means that while you have some very strong credentials, you were not considered to be as competitive as those being offered admission. However, the good news is that you were not denied. There is still a chance, and from my experience, in most cases, a very good chance you will be admitted.

   b. Don't assume you are going to be denied. As I just mentioned, most likely the opposite is true. If you stay calm, confident and patient, you will most likely get more encouraging news down the road.

   c. Make sure you follow instructions. Once again, be professional and do what is suggested or asked of you. If you do not receive any information about what to do next, ask. Don't demand, complain or argue. Just ask if there is anything you can do. If you are told no, accept that and do not do anything. It may tell you something about this institution if they do not provide you an opportunity to further address your interest in their program. If you are given specific instructions on what you can do, follow every one of them.

   Here are some of the steps you may be told to take or you may choose to take if there is something you can do:

   d. If feedback is offered, ask for it! Listen to what you are told. Do not argue, become angry, or get a chip on your shoulder. Thank the provider of the information and make sure you know how you are to respond. If a letter from you is acceptable, write one as soon as you can. Address each issue head on and explain why/how you believe you can "overcome" the concern.

e. Mount a letter of recommendation campaign. This is the time to have two or three additional individuals write recommendation letters for you. You may want some of your original recommenders to write another letter. You may ask others to do so. At most, do not send more than three or four letters of recommendation at this point. More than this is overkill.

f. Request a campus interview. If your request is granted and this is a top choice on your list, do it. If a campus interview is not made available to you and you did have an interview with an alumnus, contact him/her to see if there are any recommendations they would make. This person might even be willing to write a letter of recommendation for you.

g. Be cautiously creative. Some wait listed applicants send a CD, poem, photo album, acronym, e-card, a "Top Ten Reasons Why I Should be Admitted" list, etc. Please do not do all of these for the same institution! Choose one.

h. Write a confidential, hand-written note to the person who signed your notification letter. This could be sent a few weeks before a final decision is supposed to be sent. Indicate your level of interest in this program. Mention that you have responded as requested to your wait list status. End the note by thanking this person for the time and attention he/she has given and will give to your application.

i. Practice your skills in patience and professionalism. If ever you help admissions evaluators get a sense of you for better or worse, it is when you have been placed on the waiting list. There are several reasons for creating such a list; one reason that is not among them is that of deliberately trying to frustrate you. If you come across as being offended, inconvenienced, angry, resentful, argumentative or arrogant, you are almost certainly determining the outcome of your application – you will be denied. However, if you go with the flow, and hang in there with a positive and confident outlook, you will help yourself greatly.

j. Prepare for either admission or denial. While one decision is much easier to prepare for than the other, be ready for either response. Some suggestions on these decisions are presented next.

2. **Denied** – This is never easy. After all of the time and work you have put in to your application, it can feel like a real slap in the face. If you are extremely upset, do not react by phone or in writing right away. Give it a few days. As you reflect, consider the following:

   a. Accept the decision. At this point you cannot change it.

   b. Don't take it personally. Remember, under most circumstances the admissions committee is faced with a very difficult task: choosing a limited enrollment number from among a very large applicant pool. These individuals are good people, who are doing their best in a very difficult situation. Believe me, they are not personally against you in any way.

   c. Write a thank you note to the person who signed your notification letter. If you believe you can honestly do so, send a letter thanking the admissions director for taking the time to review your application. Perhaps that is all you will decide to do.

   d. If you believe something was missed or overlooked, ask about it. Kindly ask if your most recent test score was received or if a recent transcript is in your file. You may want to verify that all of your recommendation letters were received. If you sent a cover letter and it contained some very important information, check to be sure it was included when your application was read. On occasion something may have been overlooked. If so, most admissions committees will provide another complete evaluation. If they are unwilling to do so, or worse yet, not even willing to take another look at that part of your application, perhaps you are getting additional information about whether this is really the place for you.

e. Sometimes admissions committees make mistakes. On rare occasions, a decision to admit is accidentally entered as a denial. Please know that this rarely happens. All admissions offices have several "checks" in place to ensure that the proper decision is communicated to the applicant. But it would not hurt to check. Do so kindly, not in an accusatory way.

f. Request feedback and honor what you are told. Some admissions personnel will offer feedback for denied applicants in person, over the phone or in writing. If they do, ask for this feedback. Do not argue when you receive the feedback. Make sure you understand what was communicated, and be sure to thank the person for his/her time.

g. Ask if additional information from you could result in a second look. Perhaps you have already found this out. If not, it never hurts to ask.

h. Consider re-applying and ask about that process.

i. Remember: this is a temporary disappointment, not a final blow. You WILL succeed, even though the path right now may not be as you planned.

j. This is a practice opportunity for patience and professionalism. If you decide to respond in some way to being denied, please remember this: If you want to send a positive message to the admissions committee, it is now. A mature, thoughtful attitude makes a huge and positive impression, believe me!

**For what it's worth, I completely empathize with those who are denied admission. My first application to the doctoral program on the top of my list was denied. I was extremely disappointed and somewhat angry. So I waited a few days and then called the admissions office. I learned that my most recent standardized test score was not in my file. Also, I was told that an assessment of my academic skills did not come through in my letters of recommendation. I asked if I could send the updated test score and provide another recommendation letter. They said yes. I did so and one month later was accepted. I was even awarded one full year of coursework. I realize this may not be the outcome every time, but you never know.*

2. **Admitted** – WAY TO GO!! You did it! Your hard work has paid off. You still have lots of decisions ahead, but for now, take some time off - go and celebrate!!! Once you have "recuperated" from the euphoria, here are some next steps to consider:

   a. Thank those who helped you (family, friends, recommenders, interviewer, etc.). While you did the lion's share of the work, there are others who helped with your application and/or gave you lots of encouragement and support along the way. This may be especially true if you were initially wait listed. Be sure to thank these individuals. You might take them out for dinner, send them flowers or give them a gift certificate.

   b. Send a thank you note to the person who signed your notification letter. This goes a long way. The admissions committee works very hard too, and it is always nice to remember to say thanks to them.

   c. Read the materials you start receiving. They will contain important information about your enrollment deposit, financial aid, housing, admitted student visit programs, course scheduling, new student orientation, student life and much more. Hold on to this information and read it carefully.

   d. Start/continue talking with other admits, current students and alumni. By now you may have established contact with current or former students. You may even know others who, like yourself, have just been admitted. Reach out to these individuals. You can learn a lot from current and/or former students. You can learn a lot from future classmates as well. Knowing some of your student colleagues before you enroll is always helpful. Compare notes with them. Get their impressions of the application process you have just been through, and also of the admitted student follow-up you have been receiving so far.

   e. Try to schedule a campus visit. Whether or not you have done so already, now is a great time to visit the campus. Many institutions offer admitted student programs. This provides a great opportunity for you to meet people you may decide to join for the next few years. You may also choose to visit on your own at another time. You can always arrange a visit with the admissions staff. Here is a good tip: If you really want to get an idea of what the institution is like, make an unannounced visit. One advantage is no one knows you are coming, and you will experience things as they really are. One disadvantage is that you will not be able to schedule appointments you might want ahead of time.

f. Evaluate how you are treated post admission/deposit. As a prospective student you were in the driver's seat when deciding where you would apply. Once you submitted your application(s), you gave the wheel to the institution/admissions committee. Now that you have been admitted, you are once again in the driver's seat. You get to decide whether to accept the offer. This is a very good time to evaluate how you are treated. Does the admitted student follow-up process make you feel wanted, included and well informed? If so, great. If not, perhaps you need to think more seriously about enrollment in the program.

g. Do some comparison shopping. Remember the spreadsheet you started when initially investigating various graduate school options? Now is a good time to expand it or create a new spreadsheet. You might use the following as some of your evaluation questions:

1) How soon after I was admitted did I receive another contact from the institution?

2) Did a student or alumnus call me to offer congratulations and to offer help?

3) How often am I being contacted? It is too much? Too little?

4) How long did it take me to get an estimated annual budget?

5) Will I receive financial aid? If so, what type? Scholarships? Fellowships? Loans? Work Study? Graduate Assistantship? Stipend?

6) How much information am I receiving about courses/program of study?

7) What did I think of my campus visit post admission?

8) How friendly/helpful have the faculty, staff and students been since I was admitted?

9) Is the information I am receiving really helpful to me?

10) If I am coming with a spouse or partner, or with a family, how accommodating/inclusive is the institution?

As you did before, put the names of the institutions to which you have been admitted on the left hand column of your spreadsheet and your various evaluation questions across the top. Give each institution a grade. You will start seeing some themes emerge as you do this.

h. Start working on your financial plan. For most people this takes time. Even if you are not relocating geographically, there is a lot to consider. Make sure to read the fine print about every scholarship, fellowship, assistantship and/or stipend you are offered. If you need loan assistance, be very careful to educate yourself about all that is involved before you sign on the dotted line. One common oversight on the part of admitted students is keeping track of just how long the funds they have been awarded will last. Be sure you know whether a scholarship/fellowship/assistantship is for one year, two years, etc. This may seem elementary, but it is amazing how many incoming students make assumptions about the length of their non-loan based financial aid. Be sure you know this before you enroll. You do not want any financial surprises.

i. If you are relocating, do some preparation. Most institutions can help, but you will need to do a lot on your own. If campus housing is available, do not wait until the last minute to inquire and apply. Hopefully you have looked into this during the application process. Nonetheless, read carefully and follow directions. Yes, following directions is not over yet!

j. Keep a list of compliments/suggestions to share with the admissions office after you have enrolled. You will be exposed to the good, the bad and the very bad post admission/deposit. While things are fresh in your mind, write them down. Admissions staff members are always looking for ways to improve their service. If you are being "courted" by several institutions, make a list of "best practices" for admitted student follow up. Share these shortly after you begin your studies. You might even consider inquiring about being a student admissions volunteer or worker as part of your student experience.

**Please read the material sent to you or referred to on the web. It is extremely frustrating to prepare information for incoming students, only to have them disregard it, asking questions they could easily have answered for themselves. If you have suggestions about the way in which information is prepared or provided, definitely share those. Be careful not to create negative impressions of yourself by appearing inept at getting readily available information that has already been communicated.

Ten Tips on the Application Process:

1. Is this what YOU really want to do? If so, as much as you can, follow your own time frame and path.

2. Do not be someone you are not. It will catch up with you in the end.

3. Consider rankings, but do not focus on them as the only criteria to determine your list of options or the order of that list.

4. Take word of mouth for what it is – word of mouth.

5. Do your homework. Be prepared. Follow directions. Answer every question.

6. Remember: The evaluation process is a two-way street. As you are evaluating the institutions you are interested in, they are evaluating you. Many times the application process can be a study in human nature, for better or worse.

7. Make sure you send application materials to the right institution.

8. Be calm, assertive, and genuine.

9. Be appreciative. Say thank you. Smile.

10. Remember: In the end your success is due to YOU, not to where you studied.

Seven Deadly Sins for Applicants:

1. Rude or arrogant behavior

2. Dishonesty

3. Too much contact

4. Not following directions

5. Sending wrong or non-proofed information (essays, recommendations, etc.)

6. Asking questions you could answer for yourself

7. Leaving something completely unaddressed, or making excuses when addressing it

Seven Ways to Get Positively Noticed as an Applicant:

1. Include a succinct, upbeat cover letter with your application, stating why you are interested in the institution and why you hope they will decide to admit you.

2. If you have a strong friendship or professional relationship with a current student or a recent graduate, ask them to write a letter of recommendation for you.

3. Be creative, but not silly or outlandish.

4. Smile.

5. Stay calm/keep your cool, whatever happens.

6. Ask questions that demonstrate you did your homework and are really interested in this institution.

7. Do whatever you can as an applicant and take advantage of every opportunity provided to let the institution know you want to attend.

Deciding Where to Enroll

Now it is time to make your enrollment decision. Most institutions adhere to an enrollment deposit deadline. While they may be willing to extend it for a short period of time, they need to plan for their enrollments and respond to those who still may be on the waiting list. Do not be surprised if there is not much flexibility around the enrollment deposit deadline.

As you contemplate your decision (even if you have been admitted to just one graduate program), remember that YOU are the one going to graduate school – not someone else. Input is always helpful. You may decide to ask those whose advice you respect for their thoughts. However, in the end, it is your call. Here are some questions to ask yourself:

1. What is most important to ME when making this decision? Finances? Program Quality? Quality of Faculty? Level of Faculty interaction with students? Student Life? Location?

   **You may want to review the personal questions you answered*
   in Chapter One.

2. What is the culture of the institution? Would I enjoy it there? Remember, you are about to spend considerable time, energy and resources to earn a graduate degree. Make sure you feel reasonably comfortable about the general atmosphere you believe characterizes the institution(s) you are considering. It is not worth being unhappy for one, two or more years. Your program of study and all that goes with it will be plenty to handle in and of itself.

3. How have I been treated as an inquirer/applicant/admitted student? This is very important. Think about it. Reaching out to prospective students, applicants, and admits is very telling about the way institutions treat their students, and perhaps their alumni too. If you have not been treated very well do not assume anything is going to improve after you enroll. In fact, once you are there, what incentive is there to treat you differently than before you arrived? Your enrollment decision is not just about

the academic program. It is about where you believe you can be part of a community that cares about and wants to help each other.

4. Should I defer? Are you ready to enroll now? As you have gone through the application process your feelings may have changed, or circumstances around you may have resulted in a need to step back and determine if this is the best time to start your graduate program. For different reasons, I deferred enrollment for both my master's and doctoral program, in each case, for two years. In both instances this decision ended up being the best thing I ever did. You may be told that deferral is only granted in extreme cases. If so, you might consider withdrawing and re-applying. I have rarely seen a situation where someone who was admitted, decided to hold off for that year and re-applied, was denied.

   If you do decide to defer or withdraw, make sure you have addressed the following issues:

   a. Will any scholarship assistance I have received still be available when I do enroll?

   b. Is there an additional enrollment deposit if I defer?

   c. For how long can I defer?

   d. If I am withdrawing, what is the re-application process like?

   One other piece of advice: If you defer or withdraw, and you REALLY want to attend this institution, you will need to demonstrate that by periodically staying in touch, and following all guidelines provided to you. It would not hurt to provide a written update every four to six months detailing where you are, what you are doing and what you have done regarding the deferral or re-application process. As the admissions staff review your application folder, they will find regular updates there. This indicates to them that you mean business.

5. Should I submit an enrollment deposit to more than one institution? This is a good but tough question. If, after giving every consideration to you options, you are absolutely deadlocked between two institutions, and enrollment deposit deadlines

are approaching, you might do this. But do it for a very short amount of time. Do not send a deposit to more than two institutions. Many admissions officers compare their deposit lists. If it is discovered that you are on more than one list, you will most likely be contacted by the admissions staff and pressed for a decision. This doesn't look good for you.

By all means do not pay two deposits and just let it go! This is extremely inconsiderate, unprofessional and, some might argue, unethical. Have the courtesy and integrity to withdraw before it is too late for that institution to replace you in their incoming class.

Shortly Before Enrolling

1. Reach out to other admitted students. This is a great way to get a "jump start" on your student experience. Find out if there are "admits" who live near you. Initiate a get-together to meet them. Compare notes. Ask questions. Share information. In so doing, you will develop a network of student colleagues and friends well before orientation.

2. Review the website. About once a week log on to the website and look for new information. If there is a link for "upcoming events" or "what's new," read that section. You don't want to be surprised by anything due to your lack of preparation. Read all you can about the academic program in which you will be studying. If there is a new student or orientation website, familiarize yourself with it. Check out extra-curricular/student activities that interest you. This prevents you from being "broadsided," helps you feel like a member of the community already and definitely gives you more confidence as you prepare to matriculate.

3. Continue to look for scholarship opportunities. If finances are an issue (and for most students they are), do not stop inquiring/ learning about additional financial help. Often, the financial aid website will contain all sorts of resources for you to consider. Here is another tip: While you do not want to do this every week or even every month, periodically, you should check with the financial

aid staff to see if any institutional scholarship dollars have become available. Occasionally this happens, and it does not hurt for your name to be in their "thinking." At the same time, do not put the responsibility of finding more assistance solely on others – that is primarily your job. Do your homework and keep a positive attitude. It WILL work out financially.

4. Re-read the materials you were sent after being admitted. This is VERY IMPORTANT! When you first opened your admission letter, you were elated and did not think about much else. Then you started getting all sorts of information – a LOT of information. It is next to impossible to remember or catch everything. Designate some time once a week and for about an hour or so re-read everything you have received. If what you are reading is no longer useful (i.e., you have already paid your enrollment deposit or filled out that certain form), move on. It is amazing what you can glean from all the information you have at your disposal. Often times you find that you have missed something important.

5. Do some research about the career placement office. You have just been admitted and we are already talking about what happens after you leave! But remember, your student experience is going to go by very quickly. Just as you spent a lot of time preparing to apply, you now need to start turning your attention to what it is you are looking to do when you graduate. Some graduate students already know what they will be doing. Most are not 100% certain. Start checking out the website of the career placement office. There is a WEALTH of helpful information there. Even if you are pretty sure about what you will be doing once you earn your degree, this is the time to ask yourself, "Is this ABSOLUTELY what I want to do?" If so, great. If not, you have a tremendous resource in this office.

CHAPTER 3

GETTING OUT
(Having a Successful
Student Experience)

→

CHAPTER 3

GETTING OUT
(Having a Successful Student Experience)

Congratulations! You have started your graduate program of study. All of your hard work, preparation and planning have paid off and you are about to participate in orientation for incoming students, register for the upcoming term and head to your first class.

The work-load will be very heavy, even daunting, at times. You will have a lot of reading assignments, projects, papers, etc., to complete, and in addition, other program requirements of which to keep track. And, of course, you will need to keep up with your financial obligations. Some students will continue to work full- or part-time. Some will be adding graduate study to relationship and/or family responsibilities, while others will be leaving loved ones behind as they focus on their studies. All in all, there will be quite a bit on your shoulders.

The age range for graduate students is wide. For those of you who have more recently graduated from college, keep in mind that graduate school is NOT College. You will be expected to behave as a mature and responsible adult. While you may receive reminders from time to time from the Registrar's Office, Student Financial Services, Career Placement, etc., faculty and staff will not be overly involved in ensuring that you do what you need to do when you need to do it. It's largely up to you.

Here are some tips for ensuring a successful and personally fulfilling student experience:

1. **Allow yourself time to adjust - Relax.**

    Graduate school represents a major change in your life. Major changes, even good ones, still carry with them a certain level of stress. Some graduate students move to a new city with very few if any friends/acquaintances. Some leave a full-time job, changing their living situation, or dramatically altering their financial status. Additionally, there are the new responsibilities of graduate study. It is a lot to handle, and in the beginning it could be a bit rocky. I remember when I started my masters program. I had been out of college for two years, was a newlywed and was moving away from my home/family/friends all at the same time. I took a job filling orders in a nearby warehouse while my wife worked as a secretary. We had one car, and at the beginning our work schedules overlapped to the point that I had to walk a mile to pick up the car when I finished my shift. It was a lot to handle all at one time and for several months I felt displaced and disoriented. Gradually I adjusted to my new home, institution, job and, of course, to married life. But I have to confess, it probably would have gone a bit more smoothly if I had relaxed a bit more and gone with the flow. Seven years later, when I started my doctoral program, I had been out of graduate school for five years and for the first time in my life was taking classes on the quarter system (three academic terms per year), rather than the semester system (two academic terms per year). Also, I had left a very good paying full-time job, and was back to working part-time again. However, this time I was working with an educational consulting firm. Being a bit older and having earned one graduate degree definitely helped. I was not as stressed as I had been seven years earlier. I felt more relaxed and, as a result, made the transition more smoothly and quickly.

2. **Set priorities and stick to them.**

This is YOUR time. This is YOUR graduate degree. Determine what you want from this experience. On one side of the spectrum, some graduate students will want to spend time primarily reading, studying and doing research. They may spend a lot of time alone. On the other end of the spectrum, some students may be doing their graduate degree for more pragmatic reasons. They may not focus solely on academics. Wherever you fall on the spectrum, this is your experience. Only you can and should set the priorities. It is not a matter of a right or wrong set of priorities; it is more about what you really want to get out of this experience. That said, graduate study offers a chance to delve in to issues, ideas, authors, concepts, research and debate in ways you may never experience again. While social life is important and advancing your career admirable, do not miss the amazing opportunities you will have to broaden your horizons intellectually. Take advantage of what your professors have to offer. In addition, some of your best learning and, in many cases, some of your lifelong friendships, will come from your student colleagues.

3. **Operate with realistic expectations. Do not try and do it all, all the time.**

Very few people I know are able to do everything well all the time. As you set your priorities, be careful not to set them so high that you end up being unable to meet them and, as a result, feel liked you have failed in some way. Think realistically about what you can and cannot do. I had to work part-time during my first year of master's study and full-time during my second and final year. I was married. I had made friends with many of my classmates and wanted to spend time socializing with them. Therefore, if I was to get some rest and do all I wanted to do, I was unable to devote all of my time to studying. So I did not expect myself to get straight A's. I ended up graduating with high honors, but some of my classmates had a higher GPA than I did. That was okay with me. In my doctoral program, I worked part-time during my first two years and full-time thereafter. I went through a personal crisis in my second year of study and some other life changes in the years that followed. I was not able to devote 100% of my time to my academic program, so I lowered my expectations in that area and ended up with a few B's. However, I still graduated with high honors, having made some wonderful friends and having maintained my sanity.

4. **Do not be argumentative, but do not be a doormat either. Try to find solutions to problems, and do not expect perfection.**

No graduate institution is perfect. As you become part of your institutional community, you will most likely encounter some less than thrilling experiences and notice some "rough spots" that could/should be addressed. These could come from inside or outside of the classroom. Be careful not to be a doormat and just let things happen around you that you have the ability to help to change. At the same time, resist the temptation to respond in such a way that you are perceived as argumentative, unreasonable, a complainer or a troublemaker. Work to find realistic solutions. Here are some examples:

a. You have a class that you believe is very poorly taught/managed, and/or in which the professor exhibits arrogance, disinterest in students, weak interpersonal skills, lack of knowledge of the subject matter, etc. You believe the class is a poor investment of your time and money. If there is a request for anonymous feedback at the end of the class, be sure to respond. If you know other students share your views, encourage them to complete the survey as well. If what happened is, from your vantage point, a major issue, go to the academic support office and ask what options you have in reporting the matter to the chief academic officer.

b. You have observed poor customer service somewhere on campus or you are made aware of, or are personally affected by, a policy/procedure that does not make sense and about which you have a suggestion. Administrators welcome feedback from students when it is honest, sincere, respectful, and carries with it a realistic means for improvement. They generally want to know when things are not working, so they can try to make them better.

c. You have an idea that you believe would help make things better at your institution. Share it with appropriate individuals, perhaps with several of your fellow students. If there is a consensus that this idea would help, send a letter to the president, or chief administrator over the area about which you have an idea: academic, financial, student affairs, marketing, admissions, alumni, etc. Volunteer to help put the idea in to action.

5. **If you need help, be willing to ask for it. If something happens to you that you believe is wrong (abuse, harassment, unfair treatment), report it.**

    a. Do you believe you need some academic help? Ask. Are you struggling with stress, anxiety or depression? Reach out. Are you experiencing financial difficulties? Talk about it. Holding things in and not addressing growing issues will only result in more difficulty down the road. Toward the end of my doctoral program I took my very first Accounting course. It was extremely challenging for me. I asked the professor if I could attend both sections of the class – mine and the one he taught on weekends. He said yes. I sat in the front row, joined a study group and in the end got an A in the class. When, during my second year of doctoral study my marriage suddenly and unexpectedly came to an end, I seriously considered not completing my degree. Thanks to the love and support of many I continued on with my program of study. There were some major financial struggles along the way. However, I connected with a wonderful staff in the financial aid office and over time things worked out. Do not be too proud to ask for help when you need it. That is a sign of strength, not weakness.

    b. Are you struggling emotionally and/or psychologically? You may need to consider getting professional help. While this is sometimes hard to admit or act on once acknowledged, do not berate yourself. Speak with a trusted member of the faculty or administration at your institution, or a loved one or your physician. Get the help you need. If finances are an issue, there are many therapists whose charges are based on income. Many universities offer free counseling services for up to a certain number of visits. Be assured that just as with academic and medical information, any discussions about therapy and the therapy itself remain totally and completely confidential.

c. Have you been abused or harassed by a fellow student, faculty or staff member? Have you witnessed behavior that is completely unprofessional, inappropriate or, perhaps, illegal? Remember, you have rights and responsibilities as a member of your academic community. Check in the student handbook for policies governing appropriate conduct, abuse and harassment. Follow the procedures set forth in these policies. Your privacy is guaranteed and your confidentiality will be maintained.

d. Have you received a grade you do not believe to be fair? Remember, faculty members are not perfect. They may make a mistake or simply overlook something. If you believe you know the faculty member well enough, go and speak with her/him directly about your concerns. If not, you can consult with an academic advisor or someone on campus who is identified as a student advocate. At some institutions where I have worked this person is the student ombudsman. He/she will keep your conversation completely in confidence, but will also have some means of working out a possible solution.

6. **Be responsible. Pay your bills. Follow directions. Read.**

This piece of advice may not apply equally to all graduate students. The age range for those pursing advanced degrees varies greatly. The point here is not to look at graduate school as a re-visitation of college. The undergraduate years hopefully provide an opportunity for students to move from adolescence to young adulthood. Graduate students are expected to be fully independent and act in a responsible manner. Do not rely on others to remind you about your academic requirements, your financial responsibilities or other policies that govern your student experience. Take the initiative. READ. If something is not clear, then ask. As I mentioned earlier, do not ask questions for which the answers have already been provided. Follow directions, be proactive and take ownership of your graduate school journey.

7. **Be yourself. Do not allow yourself to be intimidated or made to feel inferior. Learn from others but don't let them dissuade you from being who you are and from pursuing what is most important to you.**

   Joining a community of fellow graduate students can be intimidating. Graduate school enrollments are lower than those of undergraduate institutions. The admissions process is most always more selective. This means that you are now rubbing elbows with some very capable, driven, committed, intelligent, enthusiastic, motivated, opinionated and goal-oriented individuals, who are ready and willing to do what it takes to succeed. But keep this in mind: You were also admitted to be a member of your academic community. The admissions committee saw in you what it did in your fellow classmates. Be confident of your talents and abilities, of your thoughts and ideas. Learn from those around you, but do not allow yourself to feel inferior or that you do not also have something to contribute. Stay true to your goals and to following what is important to you, just as your fellow students are doing.

8. **Continue to look for financial assistance.**

   Do not stop looking for additional funding opportunities. Check with your department once each quarter/semester/term to see if any additional fellowships or assistantships have been approved. Check with the financial aid office to see if there are any new scholarships available. Find out if any work-study positions have opened up on campus that are conducive to your schedule. Check the web for outside funding opportunities. You may want to schedule a specific time every few weeks to research this.

9. **Take advantage of the career placement office.**

   Some graduate students may already have their future employment confirmed when they begin their studies. Most do not. That is why there is a career placement office on campus. Take advantage of the resources of this office right from the start. Do not wait until six months before graduation to reach out. The staff is ready, willing and able to assist you with a host of services, including resume preparation, interviewing preparation, information on potential employers, "meet the recruiters" events and so much more. Take this service seriously. After all, you are paying for it.

10. **Resist the temptation to cheat, plagiarize or embellish in order to get ahead.**

Of all the pitfalls to avoid, this is it. Do not risk your future by yielding to the temptation to be unethical in some way. YOU DO NOT NEED TO DO IT! Your success in life ultimately depends on conducting yourself with honesty and integrity. As a child, I was taught to believe the following: "Be sure your sin will find you out." Later in my life someone said to me, "Don't do something today that you'd be uncomfortable reading as a news headline tomorrow." This advice has served me well. It has been sad for me to watch students with great promise throw their futures away because of a momentary lapse in judgment, making a decision to cheat, embellish or falsely cite someone else's work as their own. The temptation is definitely there, so do not be hard on yourself if you experience a thought about being dishonest. You are human. Anyone with an ounce of integrity would readily acknowledge that they have been tempted to engage in some sort of wrongdoing. But as they say, "Just say no!"

One other piece of advice: If you do engage in wrongdoing and are caught, come clean right away. Own up to what you did and admit that you were wrong. This does not mean there will not be a consequence. However, be assured that whoever has to decide the consequence will be far more sympathetic toward someone who comes clean than toward someone who refuses to acknowledge the truth about his/her actions

11. **Do not stop having fun and do not forget important relationships outside the classroom.**

The pressures of graduate school can be great. There is endless studying, numerous deadlines, a desire to get good grades, preparation for career next steps, financial concerns and more. It is important that you take time to smell the roses and do things that are fun and enjoyable. Take a break. Go out for a bite to eat. Take in a movie or theatre performance.

Attend a sporting event. Do some volunteer work. Get away for the weekend. There were times in my graduate school journey when just taking a walk along Lake Michigan was extremely beneficial. The bottom line is, do not forget that all work and no play is not a good way to operate.

In addition, take time to maintain, strengthen and build personal relationships. Perhaps you have a spouse, partner, significant other, children, etc., who are part of your graduate school experience. Remember that they too are affected by all of this. Be appreciative of their willingness to support you and make sacrifices so you can do what you are doing. Make time for these important individuals. Do not take advantage of them. Let them participate in your student life experience. Bring them to a social event at the institution. Or, perhaps there are spouse or partner groups with which they could become involved.

Be willing to sacrifice as well. I know whereof I speak: I was a newlywed when I started my master's degree program. There were times when my marriage relationship needed to take precedence over my life as a student. Balancing things was not always easy and I did not always get it right. But that did not stop me from trying.

12. **Do not obsess about grades, ranking and reputation of your institution. In the end it is most about who you are and what you bring to the table.**

Success in life is not directly correlated with one's grade point average or with the ranking/prestige of his/her institution. Employers are going to be most interested in who you are and how strong a match they believe you are to what they are looking for. Believe me, while academic performance is a consideration, it is not the final deal maker/breaker by any means. Also, rankings will definitely fluctuate; they rarely stay the same. Focus on doing your best with integrity. Work hard and be confident of yourself and your abilities.

In Chapter One I stated the following: ". . .there are only two qualities you need to succeed, which come from within." They are PERSISTENCE and DETERMINATION. As former President Calvin Coolidge stated, these qualities are "omnipotent."** In the end, becoming proficient at the skills of persistence and determination will get you where you really want to go.

13. **This too shall pass. It is not forever and it will go by very quickly.**

There will be days when you will have second thoughts about your decision to pursue graduate study. You will encounter some difficulties along the way. Individuals with whom you have to associate will provide major challenges. Your personal life will have its ups and downs. You will feel tired, overwhelmed and discouraged at times. But know this: You are not alone. This is normal. It is part of the graduate school experience and IT WILL PASS! I know of very few who look back on their graduate school experience with regret, or with a sense that it took too long. When I sat with my fellow students on graduation day, I could not believe how fast the time had gone. All the hard work had paid off. It will for you too. Hang in there, do not lose heart and do your best to follow that age-old suggestion to "TAKE ONE DAY AT A TIME." I often say, "Just Today." That is all you have. You cannot go back and you cannot fast forward. Just take each day as it comes. You will get though this without a doubt.

14. **Do you need to take some time off? Move from full-time to part-time or visa versa? Stop your program of study entirely?**

Life is unpredictable and can take us down a very unexpected path without warning. Attending graduate school does not prevent the vicissitudes of life from occurring. There are times when you may be forced to think about changing your plans. These situations could include a financial crisis, medical emergency, academic difficulties, loss of loved one, a relationship change, new job opportunity, etc. In my case, I deferred my enrollment at both my masters and doctoral institutions because of an unexpected employment opportunity. I changed my date of completion while enrolled at both institutions, once again, due to unexpected employment offers. My course plan while completing doctoral study was also affected when I went through an unexpected divorce.

If you need to change your plans, do so. It may result in having to take a longer period of time to complete your degree. But do not lose your focus. Be patient, do what you have to do to take care of yourself and appropriately manage your responsibilities. The administrators at your institution have worked with many students whose plans need to change for shorter or longer periods of time. They will work with you to help determine the best way to proceed.

There are some cases when you may decide that you need to withdraw permanently from your program of study. Perhaps the program is not what you wanted or expected, despite your best attempts to make sure it was. Perhaps your personal situation has evolved in such a way that any form of graduate study for the foreseeable future is not an option. Perhaps you have discovered that graduate study and you are just not a match. This could be extremely disappointing, discouraging and disconcerting. You were moving in one direction, feeling perfectly confident that this was the right thing to do and now you are coming to believe that it is not. You may have left full-time employment, moved to another part of the country/world and brought loved ones with you. As you make this decision, you will most certainly be communicating with loved ones who need to be included. In addition, speak with the administrators at your institution and perhaps with a trusted friend and/or therapist. Make sure you have covered all the bases and thought things through clearly and carefully before making your decision. If you do withdraw permanently, you do so with the knowledge that you started graduate school believing it was the right thing. When you realized it was not you did what you needed to do. You should also withdraw knowing that many have done the exact same thing, and have been just fine. Finally, you will never have to wonder, "If only I'd taken the chance and gone to graduate school."

15. You can do it. I did.

You need to know that I believe higher education has made all the difference in my time on this earth. It opened doors for me personally, intellectually, relationally and vocationally, thus enriching my life in ways I never thought possible. My childhood was spent in a family/religious culture that did not value thought, discussion, curiosity, debate, disagreement or challenge. Going to a liberal arts college was not an option for me. My siblings and I were required to attend extremely conservative and fundamental religious institutions. There was little, if any, financial support when it came time for us to do so.

When I made the decision to pursue graduate study (even at a "Christian" institution) I was questioned by a parent who expressed concerns that I would lose my religious beliefs. However, the complete opposite occurred. Master's and then doctoral study literally opened my eyes and my mind. I learned to think for myself, to trust and express myself intellectually, to carry on a debate, to disagree, to speak my mind and to step outside my comfort zone. While I moved away from many of the religious beliefs I had been taught as a boy, I came to develop my own world view, which was more meaningful than anything I had known before.

Starting graduate school was extremely exciting yet, at the same time, extremely daunting. For the first time in my life I was interacting with students and faculty members who were challenging me to think, debate, study, learn and be comfortable with the idea that there may not be an answer for everything or that there was more than one answer for the same question. I felt like a sponge, asking the question "Why?" more than anything else. At times I felt empowered, confused, discouraged, excited, angry and exhilarated. But most of all I felt free. The world of knowledge, discovery, thought, inquiry and study lay at my feet and I took hold with everything I could muster. What a ride!

Upon applying for both graduate and post-graduate study, I had to do some extra work to get admitted. In the case of my master's degree, I was asked to complete extra undergraduate coursework in math and science. In the case of my doctoral program, as I mentioned in Chapter Two, I was initially denied admission. However, I contacted the admissions office and was given a chance to provide additional information to the admissions committee, which resulted in my being admitted. How grateful I am for the opportunities that were given to me to pursue educational goals and prove myself.

These opportunities emerged because I sought them; I did not have connections that opened doors. I opened my own doors, worked hard, have sought to be honest and to be a man of my word. Today I have close to 30 years of successful work in higher education as part of my life experience. I did it, not without difficulty, pain, loss, disappointment or unexpected delays. But I did it and you can too!! If I can, anybody can!!

** "Nothing in this world can take the place of persistence. Talent will not: nothing is more common than unsuccessful people with talent. Genius will not: unrewarded genius is almost a proverb. Education will not: the world is full of educated derelicts. Persistence and determination alone are omnipotent. The slogan 'press on' has solved and will always solve the problems of the human race."

- Calvin Coolidge
30th President of the United States
1872-1933

CHAPTER 4

FREQUENTLY ASKED QUESTIONS

CHAPTER 4

FREQUENTLY ASKED QUESTIONS

This final chapter addresses many of the questions I have been asked most often over the years by those thinking about, applying for and pursuing graduate study. I have organized the questions based on the three earlier chapters in the book: Inquiry Questions, Application Questions, and Student Questions. *Here we go.*

Inquiry Questions

1. **Is a graduate education really worth it? Do I get that much more from earning a masters or doctoral degree?**

   Response: There are all sorts of benefits from earning a graduate degree, including personal, educational, intellectual, emotional, financial, professional, and more. The person who best can answer this question for you IS you. How much do you want a graduate degree, and why? Bottom line, success in life is about who you are and what you do with what you have been given. You can most certainly be successful without a graduate degree. Perhaps the question to answer is, "Will I be in a position to better accomplish the goals I have set for myself by earning a graduate degree?"

2. What if my first choice institution at the start of my research moves way down on my list, based on the spreadsheet I created?

Response: Congratulations! You are doing your homework and honestly trying to determine, based on your list of important criteria, which institutions are the best options for you. Remember, it is about trying to find the best match between you and what you are looking for in an educational option. Based on your research and the honest assessment you have given your options, the new first choice institution is a better match for you. And that is what this is all about – finding the best option for YOU.

3. What if the institution I end up with as my first choice is not as prestigious as some other institutions on my list?

Response: Long-term success is not directly correlated with the prestige factor of your institution. No doubt about it, prestige may open a few more doors, but keeping them open is all up to you. Being an outstanding worker, with persistence and determination, opens doors too – more than you may realize. Hard work always pays off – always.

4. What if some important people in my life are discouraging me from going to graduate school?

Response: Why are they trying to discourage you? Do you believe any of their reasons are valid? If so, do you believe you have a valid response? How well do you know these individuals? If they are loved ones or friends you trust, then you do yourself a service to listen. However, they also need to do you the service of listening to what you have to say. In the end this is your life, so hopefully you will not be in a position some day of having to ask, "What if I'd gone ahead with my dream of a graduate education?"

5. **What if I am thinking about this more for the credential/financial rewards than for the purely educational/intellectual benefits?**

> *Response:* Join the club! Many, many individuals do not pursue a graduate degree just for the intellectual stimulation or because they desire to learn more. Many are looking for increased financial opportunities and career growth and there is nothing wrong with that. However, do not forget the amazing educational experience that awaits you as a graduate student – it is truly one of a kind.

6. **What if I have a really bad experience with an admissions representative, current student, faculty member, alumnus, etc., on the phone or in person during a campus visit/recruitment event? Either they are extremely rude to me, or we become engaged in some sort of an argument and I say something I should not, or both?**

> *Response:* My first piece of advice is not to do anything for at least 24 hours. Calm down; sleep on it and then act. If you believe something you said or did was inappropriate, contact ONLY the individual to whom you want to apologize and do so in person or on the phone. I do not suggest putting the apology in writing. If you believe someone behaved in an inappropriate manner toward you, you should certainly feel free to contact the director of admissions and make a formal complaint. Some individuals may not hesitate to do this and feel completely within their rights to make known what happened. Others may decide that they do not want to say anything for fear that it could affect the outcome of their application. This is a personal choice. However, having been in situations where complaints were made about a member of my staff, a student host, an alumni interviewer, etc. by an applicant, I can honestly say that such complaints NEVER resulted in that person's application being given anything but the most thorough review possible to ensure that a fair and equitable decision was made.

7. If I substitute the name of another institution, the marketing information on the web, in a video, or on the printed page basically sounds the same – just a varied ordering of copy, and different visual images/graphics. How can I trust what I read on the web or in printed materials?

> *Response:* As with any type of advertising, institutions want to put their best foot forward. They do so by using words, phrases and clichés that sound very familiar. Do not be surprised by this. If you dig deeper, you will be able to start making some helpful comparisons. For instance, get a list of a few recent graduates from the program to which you are applying and contact them. What do these individuals have to say (Remember, they are no longer enrolled so they can be completely candid with you.) Did they get what they came for? What about the faculty – how well known are they? How recently have they been published? Once admitted, get information on how their classes have been evaluated in the past two years. Get a list of the top five recruiters of graduates from the institution. What do they have to say about the quality of education? And last but not least, visit the campus if at all possible. What did YOU observe? How were YOU treated? How did YOU fit in? Overall, how did YOU feel? The way one feels during a campus visit is usually how one feels as a student on the campus.

8. At what point does an institution move from being wonderfully responsive to me, and start looking too desperate to recruit me?

> *Response:* As the competition for graduate students increases, so does the level of contact institutions will have with them. It may be a bit difficult to distinguish between genuine interest and overkill. But do your best to follow your gut. Does the contact seem reasonable? Are you being contacted more than once per week (that might be a bit excessive)? Are the contacts made to you varied and do they contain new and helpful information? Are folks respectful of you? Are those contacting you upbeat, but not begging you to enroll all the time? Are they careful not to speak unkindly or inappropriately about other options you may be considering? More selective institutions tend to recruit less. But that is a very general statement. Almost everyone has stepped into the recruitment ring these days. There is competition at all levels, even at the most selective institutions.

9. Am I making a mistake if I eliminate an option before applying?

> *Response:* No, not if you are convinced it is not what you are looking for.

10. What if my finances are just not adding up? What if going to graduate school seems economically impossible?

> *Response:* This is definitely something to consider, no doubt about it. It is helpful if you have at least one year's tuition "in the bank" before you enroll. Make sure you know what financial aid you can receive, including loans, scholarships, assistantships, fellowships, work-study, etc. Do some financial planning. You might consider meeting with a financial advisor, or with trusted relatives, loved ones and/or friends. Cover all the bases – do not leave anything to chance. Make sure you know that you can cover what you need to cover. Do not enroll if you have not planned, to the best of your ability, for the financial responsibilities you are about to assume.

Application Questions

1. **Does what I do during the application process really make that much of a difference? Isn't the decision making process based more on quotas and "who you know" than on genuinely admitting the best applicants?**

   Response: The answer to both questions is yes. Most institutions are definitely trying to achieve certain enrollment goals – quality, diversity and a strong acceptance percentage, to name a few. Within the bounds of the law they try very hard to achieve these goals. There are times when who an applicant knows at a certain institution could have an impact on the application decision. However, it has been my experience time and time again that the manner with which applicants represent themselves can and does make a difference. Well written essays, a strong cover letter and a solid interview do help to narrow the competition. Always look to put your best foot forward. Try to relax; remember that things do work out the way they are meant to.

2. **What if I discover an error in my application after I've already submitted it?**

   Response: Don't panic. Contact the admissions office and calmly explain what happened. Do not ask the admissions office to make any corrections or changes. Rather, ask if you can send updated/corrected information via overnight mail. If the admissions office offers to make changes or corrections, and that can readily be done, accept the offer with your thanks. Then send a thank you note to the person who helped you. Before ending the conversation, be sure you have done the following: 1) Know exactly how/when the corrections/changes will be made; 2) Thank the admissions staff for their patience and assistance; 3) Ask if you should call to confirm that the corrections/changes have been made; 4) Get the name of the person who is assisting you.

If you are sending corrected/updated information via overnight mail, make sure to enclose a note indicating with whom you spoke, and once again, thank the admissions staff for their patience and assistance. Do not be overly apologetic or dramatic. We all make mistakes. If you handle things calmly and do not over-react, you may help yourself by demonstrating to the admissions committee how you handle a difficult and potentially embarrassing situation.

3. **What if I have a bad experience with the admissions staff, while on a campus visit, or with an interview?**

Response: As I suggested (if this happens before applying), wait 24 hours before doing anything. Then, if you believe you were the offending party, apologize in person or on the phone and follow up with a written apology. This time, however, copy the director of admissions on your letter. That way what you said in the letter will directly reach the director, and not be communicated second hand. If you believe you have been offended or treated inappropriately, contact the director of admissions only, and do so in writing. Send your letter overnight mail, and indicate that the contents of the letter are confidential. Inform her/him of your complaint, provide your contact information and ask to speak with her/him about this matter as soon as possible. If you have not heard from anyone within three days and you know that your letter did reach its destination, call and ask to speak with the director. The response you receive to your complaint will tell you something about the institution to which you have applied. Again, in most cases a bad experience does not have a huge impact on the final decision provided you have handled yourself honestly, calmly and professionally. Once again, a situation like this, as difficult as it may be, provides insight into who you are and how you behave in situations that are not optimal.

4. **What if I decide that, for whatever reason, I am no longer interested in an institution I have applied to before they have notified me of a decision?**

> *Response:* You have been doing your homework and have one less option on the list. Just send a letter to the admissions director, asking that your application be withdrawn. Or you might decide to wait and see what the decision is on your application. After all, you did do all the work and the application fee is non-refundable.

5. **What if several days have gone by since the notification deadline and I have not heard anything?**

> *Response:* My best advice is to wait at least one week after the notification deadline. If you have not heard anything, call the admissions office and ask for an update.

6. **What if I discover that another applicant falsified his/her application in some way?**

> *Response:* This is a tough one. You have two choices: Leave it alone or report the applicant to the admissions director. In the end, this is a personal choice. There is not a right or wrong way to respond. Some may believe they have a moral obligation to report the applicant; others may believe they should not do so. If you do choose to report, I suggest you do so in writing, have absolute proof of your claim and that you identify yourself. Claims made anonymously are generally considered less credible. Obviously, if you have reason to believe that the applicant you want to report could learn it was you who reported them and, therefore, you could be in danger, do not identify yourself. However, explain why you are not doing so.

7. What if I learn one of my recommenders did not speak well of me?

Response: If your information is absolutely true, you may have a problem. It is generally assumed that applicants would ask individuals to recommend them because they are confident the recommendation will be positive. A negative recommendation is usually a red flag. My suggestion is that you ask another person if they would be willing to provide a positive recommendation for you and then ask the admissions director if it is possible to add this recommendation to your file before a final decision is made. While the negative recommendation is a concern, the way you handle the situation will provide the admissions director and the admissions committee with additional information about you. In some cases applicants who initially received a negative recommendation, but who handled the situation well, were admitted.

Some applicants have asked whether it would be useful to provide a letter to the admission director addressing the negative recommendation. While such a letter will offer background information and the context that will help provide some explanation for what happened, I do not recommend doing this. If the applicant can provide an explanation of why they think the recommendation was negative, the major question on the minds of the admissions committee would be, "Then why did you ask this person to recommend you in the first place?" The only time I would think a letter like this would be useful is if the applicant learned something after the fact that he/she did not know when first asking the person for a recommendation. In that case, I would suggest sending an explanation letter immediately, along with another recommendation that is sure to be positive. If you have an idea of what was communicated of a negative nature, ask the new recommender to address that very issue, providing a more positive evaluation of you in that area.

8. What if, after I have applied and before a decision is made, something major happens in my life that I believe could help my chances of being admitted?

> *Response:* It is important to recognize what type of event is defined as "major." A promotion, job change, special award or recognition, etc. are major events that an admissions committee may want to know about. By all means communicate this to the committee. Do so in writing and alert the admissions office that you are sending updated information. Send it via overnight mail. Let the admissions committee know you believe this new information supports your belief that you are a viable applicant for the program. Offer to provide additional information or answer any additional questions. Be confident but not arrogant.

9. At what point does my genuine interest in an institution move from being reasonable to being unreasonable or appearing desperate?

> *Response:* Responding to questions that are asked of you by the admissions office, updating your application with important, major information, correcting a mistake, or responding to a bad recommendation are reasonable and acceptable forms of contact. Calling every week, asking several others to call or write on your behalf, sending several notes or letters, or trying to be overly funny or unique, is overkill. If you have communicated effectively in your application, and have had contact when necessary, you have done your job well. More than this is too much and will most likely backfire.

10. **What if I am admitted to an institution that offers me a greater financial incentive to enroll than my first choice institution, to which I have also been admitted and offered financial assistance?**

> *Response:* You have a very interesting decision to make. Bottom line: Finances are important, but should not be the primary influencer of your enrollment decision. In the end, you should enroll where you believe there is the best fit for you. As suggested earlier, financial planning will allow you some flexibility in this regard. But, at the same time, if you believe the program offering you the most in financial assistance will give you what you are looking for, consider that program seriously. One other idea: You may want to contact your first choice institution, asking if additional funding has become available. Some believe it is acceptable to let the institution know what you were offered elsewhere. I do not support that strategy. It can easily be perceived that you are only concerned about the financial implications of graduate study. Some institutions could make a note of that and you could be looked over for additional funding down the road. However, asking if any other funding has become available is not considered an inappropriate question. The only time I would suggest you share what you have been offered elsewhere is if you are specifically asked to do so. Then you are simply responding to a question, not looking like you are all and only about the money.

Admit Questions

1. **What if I have positive and/or negative feedback about the application process for the admissions office?**

   Response: Now is a great time to provide it. You have been admitted and should feel free to provide feedback. Many institutions conduct surveys of their admitted students – you might ask if you will be receiving one. Whether or not you do, feel free to reach out and share your thoughts. Ask to speak with someone in person, or have a phone conversation. Or you could put your thoughts in writing to the director of admissions.

   As an admissions director, it was always extremely helpful for me to hear feedback from admitted students. After all, they had made it successfully through the application process. Their insights were coming based on a positive application decision. Some of the best input I received came from "admits."

2. **When will I be able to speak to an academic advisor?**

   Response: Hopefully your admission letter will include information about "next steps," i.e., financial aid notification, campus visit programs, orientation, registration and academic advising. There will also most likely be a website for newly admitted students. If you do not see anything in your admission letter or on the web, reach out to the admissions office, asking about the advising process and how best to reach/communicate with your advisor.

3. **When is an appropriate time for me to reach out to faculty members?**

> *Response:* Reaching out to faculty is something you could probably do at any time. However, please keep in mind the following: 1) They may be on leave, or taking a sabbatical (which means they are on paid leave). Hopefully this would be indicated via a voicemail answering message or with an automated email response. 2) When they are in residence, they are extremely busy and the response you get may vary. If you do not hear from a faculty member at all or you do hear back, but the response is not very informative or welcoming, do not take it personally. If you do not hear back, do not initiate contact again. If you end up enrolling at the institution, most faculty members post open office hours. My experience has been that they make a commitment to meet with students during these times. In-person contact with faculty is always best. So do not get discouraged if initial email or phone communication is not successful.

4. **When will I be notified about financial aid? Should I use a financial aid offer from one institution to leverage an award, or higher award, at another institution?**

> *Response:* You should receive financial aid information during the application process and most definitely after being admitted. Some institutions notify you of your financial aid award at the time you are admitted. Others wait for a period of time before notifying you. Also, you may hear about scholarship awards before you hear about loans. Loan information usually has to wait to be communicated until the complete student budget has been prepared. The time frame for doing this varies greatly. Once again, check the admitted student website for information on financial aid notification. If you do not see anything there or, if what you do see is not helpful, contact the admissions office.

> As for using one award to leverage another, only you can know if you believe this is right or not. I do not encourage this. Ideally, the decision to enroll in graduate school should be made based on many factors, not just based on financial aid.

Even if you do not receive all that you had expected or hoped for you should keep in mind all of the research you did before and during the application process. The clear best option for you may not end up offering you the largest financial aid package. Trying to "negotiate" the best financial aid deal can backfire. It can make you look greedy - like you are not really interested in the intellectual, interpersonal and professional benefits of graduate study. I would not try to leverage a better financial aid package before enrolling. However, I would consider making an appointment with the financial aid office after matriculating and state my case at that time. This shows that while I am definitely able to communicate financial need, I am also and primarily committed to my educational and career goals.

5. What if I want to defer my enrollment?

Response: Many students do this - I was one of them. I deferred for both my master's and doctoral program. However, there were genuine extenuating circumstances that occurred after my admission that led me to request deferral. Ideally you should apply for the term you really plan to start. But, if something comes up that causes you to believe holding off is the best option, do not hesitate to ask about this. Most institutions have deferral policies. In most cases, you can defer for only one year. Often you will be asked to pay an additional enrollment deposit, which is non-refundable. This is their way of making sure you are really serious about joining the student body in the future. In some rare cases, you cannot defer. Rather, you are instructed to withdraw and re-apply. Should this be the policy, while I cannot predict the outcome, I have rarely seen a situation where an admitted student, who withdrew and re-applied, clearly explaining the reasons for that course of action, was not offered re-admission.

One final point about deferral: If you are awarded a scholarship or fellowship, make sure you find out if this award is still available to you if you defer. Sometimes the award will be waiting for you; other times it will not.

6. **What do I do if I have been admitted to two institutions; one has offered me financial aid already, but wants an enrollment deposit before I have heard about my financial aid package from the other institution? What do I do, especially if I need financial aid and the other institution is my first choice?**

> *Response:* Do not panic. Things will work out for you the way they were meant to if you have done all you can and you keep believing in your dreams (this may sound very philosophical, but trust me, it is true!). If you are waiting to hear from another option, ask for an extension on the other deposit deadline. All admissions officers are familiar with this dilemma, and most are very willing to offer an extension.

7. **What about others affected by my pursuing graduate study? Spouse? Partner? Children? Parents? Employer?**

> *Response:* Hopefully, this not the first time you are asking this question. By now you have been discussing your plans with loved ones who will be most impacted by your decision to pursue graduate study and they are supporting you. You need to make plans for your actual transition. If there are re-location matters, it would be best to start discussing them and making plans accordingly. Do you and/or a loved one need to seek employment? Do you need to look for daycare/schooling for children? Do you need to make sure things are in place for aging or ailing parents? And, of course, if you are leaving your current employer, you need to inform her/him. Some admitted students have already discussed their desire to go to graduate school with their employers. In some cases, the employer may be helping to pay for tuition, etc., with an understanding that the employee will return after graduation. In other cases, going to graduate school means completely cutting ties with an employer. Whatever your situation, do your best to ensure that your boss is informed that you are leaving in plenty of time.

> In some cases, there may be a less than productive relationship between you and your employer. Once again, do all you can to leave in the right way. That may be hard to do but, in the end, it is the best way all around.

8. Should I invest in health insurance at the institution?

> *Response:* Most institutions have reasonably good health insurance plans. Obviously, the decision about where to invest in health insurance will depend on the number of options you have. If you and/or a loved one will both be working, you may be fully covered by one or both employers. However, if you are not sure how things will play out with job opportunities, you may be wise to invest in your institution's health insurance plan, at least for the first term or first year. You can always cancel if you find you no longer need it.

9. If I am re-locating, what if I want to move early?

> *Response:* For some individuals this is the way to go. Moving early allows you to settle in a bit and get used to your new living arrangements before you start classes. If you are going to be working, you may have a chance to start your job. If you will be living in campus housing, however, you may not have as easy a time moving in much before the start of your term of enrollment because many institutions use breaks in the academic calendar to perform maintenance on their residential facilities. This is especially true during the summer months.

10. What if I'm feeling extremely nervous about my ability to succeed and these feelings intensify as my enrollment date gets closer?

> *Response:* I would be more concerned if you were not feeling this way. Keep in mind that you are undergoing a major change in your life and taking on major responsibilities. You are joining other students who, like yourself, are highly motivated, capable, confident and ready to jump in to their studies. While this is very exciting, it can be very daunting. If you are re-locating, do not have unlimited financial resources, were not the best student in college, etc., you will no doubt have second thoughts. This is quite normal. Try to focus on the fact that you were admitted, which means you were/are perceived as being able to handle your program of study. It will be a bit rough at times - this is certain. However, many have gone before you with varying types of challenges/worries and they did great things. So will you!

Student Questions

1. What if my program of study is not what I thought it would be and I am losing interest?

> *Response:* Is this just a temporary feeling? If so, this can happen from time to time. I would not worry too much. However, if the feeling persists and you are having some strong reservations about the program, I would suggest these two things: 1) Speak with your academic advisor and/or a trusted faculty or staff member. Also speak with a trusted friend and/ or loved one. Get their thoughts and insights. Perhaps you will decide to stick with it for a bit longer. Or, perhaps there is another program at the institution that has caught your attention and you want to consider transferring. I did that in the first year of my master's program and it worked out very well; 2) Consider taking a break from your studies to re-assess things. This may be hard to do. You may be concerned that others will view this as some sort of failure. Or, you may believe you are failing in some way. Quite the contrary. If you are fairly certain that this is just not working out, you could be wasting time, energy and money pursuing something that is not going to be useful to you. Taking a "time out" could help you to sort things through. You can always return (in a reasonable time frame), pursue another graduate degree option or choose not to continue your graduate studies at all.

2. What if I am enjoying the subject matter, but find the faculty or students to be less impressive than I expected?

Response: Are you sure this is a general feeling? Or, is it just a class or two that does not meet your expectations? If you have serious concerns about a faculty member, you do have the option of speaking with your academic advisor or with the head administrator of the academic division. Some students are concerned about doing this for fear that somehow they will be found out and "punished" in some way. If you ask that your comments remain confidential, they will. You may be doing a service to the institution by sharing your concerns. As for your fellow students, perhaps you have not yet met any with whom you are compatible. One way to meet like-minded students might be to join a student organization; another is to attend a special event, such as a symposium or lecture. You may even consider helping to start a student organization. Your student affairs staff can help you in that regard. Most students I have known eventually have met classmates with whom they connected.

3. What if I observe a fellow student cheating in some way?

Response: Whatever you do is a personal decision. Does your institution have some sort of student conduct code? If so, you have the right to follow the guidelines spelled out therein. If not, you need to decide what you believe is best. Should you decide to come forward with your claim, I suggest you do so in person to the appropriate member of the administration. I would not suggest putting your claim in writing. While some choose to make their claim in an anonymous letter, this is generally viewed by the administration as less credible.

4. **What if I start to feel depressed, discouraged, overly stressed and under incredible pressure?**

> *Response:* You are not alone. You are not weak. You are not inferior. Many students experience feelings of depression, discouragement and anxiety, or become stressed out. If these feelings last a day or two and then return to normal you should be okay. However, if these feelings persist, you need to acknowledge to yourself that you are having difficulty and reach out for help. Most institutions have a trained counselor on staff or can recommend one to you. While there may have been a time when depression, anxiety, or emotional turmoil was viewed less sympathetically, it is rarely the case now. Do not ignore these feelings until they are out of control. Reach out for help. You are exercising strength in doing so. Help is available and your communication with a counselor or therapist will be kept in the strictest of confidence. You should be able to continue with your studies if you act immediately and address whatever issues you are experiencing. Remember: It is the strong who face difficulties and try to work them out.

5. **What if the program in which I am enrolled is discontinued?**

> *Response:* Unfortunately, this does happen from time to time. Soon after I enrolled in my Ph.D. program (Higher Education Administration), I learned that it was going to be discontinued. Fortunately, I had the opportunity to continue taking classes in the program, and get most of what I needed before finishing my coursework. Rarely is a program completely discontinued when students are still enrolled and taking classes. Most likely, courses will be kept in the curriculum until all students who wish to have registered for them and no new students are admitted. Ultimately, discontinuing a program should not affect current students in that program.

6. **What if I reach the place where I am completely depleted of financial resources and am not sure I can continue in my program?**

> *Response:* Once again, you are not alone. Speak with your academic advisor and the financial aid office. Find out if there are any additional scholarship or loan opportunities. If there are, you may be able to work something out and stay enrolled. If not, you may need to take a break for one or two terms to get your finances in order. You can return and finish provided you do so in a reasonable time frame. Many students take a break for various reasons, finances being one of the major precipitators.

> If you have been enrolled full-time, you may consider finishing your degree on a part-time basis, and work full-time. Or, you may consider working at the institution you are attending so that you are close by and would most likely qualify for a tuition exemption. In both my masters and doctoral programs I worked full-time where I was attending. I did this in the final year of coursework for both programs. It was a tremendous help.

7. **What if I have an extremely negative employment interview experience?**

> *Response:* As we discussed earlier regarding a negative experience during the application process, wait 24 hours before doing anything. If you believe you are the innocent party, contact your career services staff and ask for guidance on how to proceed. These individuals will have great insight and can provide you with very helpful input. This will not be the first time they have dealt with a situation like this. By all means, let them help you. If you are the offender, contact the person with whom the incident occurred and apologize.

> The best way to do this is in person or by telephone, not in writing. You might also check in with the career services office to apprise them of the situation, as they have an ongoing relationship to maintain with employers. Remember, this is another opportunity to demonstrate your skills in handling difficult and possibly embarrassing situations. One last thing: Do not let yourself be the offender more than once. Word travels fast; you could hurt yourself far beyond the immediate situation if you become labeled a troublemaker.

8. **What if I repeatedly observe rude or inappropriate behavior by one or more of the student service offices? By the faculty? By the administration?**

> *Response:* Depending upon the exact nature of the behavior, you do have options. If the issue is poor service, go to the director/supervisor/manager of the respective department and let her/him know what happened. If what you have observed is a regular occurrence, you have spoken with the director, and it seems that nothing is being done about it, contact the respective vice president in charge of that area. If your concerns are for something other than poor service, most institutions have very clear policies regarding harassment and other forms of inappropriate behavior. You have every right to follow those policies. Most institutions also employ a student ombudsman, whose sole responsibility is to meet with students, hear their concerns and help find a resolution. Meetings with the student ombudsperson are strictly confidential. You should feel free to request a meeting with this individual at any time.

9. **What if I have an idea that, if implemented, I believe will make a huge positive difference in my student experience?**

> *Response:* By all means, share it! Most managers/directors welcome helpful feedback. I know I did. Many of the programming changes my staff and I implemented came as the result of student feedback. I remember a student coming to my office one fall afternoon to suggest that I add a short but personal note to the notification letter for admitted students. I started doing so and have continued to this day. The positive feedback I have received has been amazing.

10. **What if I do not find the courses I need to take available or there is little or absolutely no academic advising available?**

> *Response:* This can be extremely frustrating and is a matter that must be addressed. It is very possible that the administration is not aware of the problem. I suggest meeting with the head of your academic department as a first step. If you have already done so, or if you have concerns about meeting with this person, then arrange a meeting with the person to whom the department head reports. Also, you have the right to speak with the student ombudsman about this. If you believe your concerns are not being taken seriously or that the response you have received is not acceptable, I suggest putting your concerns in writing to the president. I do not usually recommend contacting the president – in many cases students do this as a first, rather than as a last step. However, your course of study is one of the primary reasons you chose the institution you did. You have the right to expect that your academic needs will be reasonably accommodated. If this is not happening and you have tried unsuccessfully to resolve the problem, this is one time the president needs to hear about it.

A Final Word:

> Well, there you have it: Your Road Map for Graduate Study. May you be successful in every area of your life, and most especially, should you decide to pursue a graduate degree. My very best to you!

> To order more books please visit my website at: **www.gradschoolroadmap.com**